LESSING

Part One

LESSING'S LIFE

LESSING

by

H. B. GARLAND, M.A., Ph.D.

FOLCROFT LIBRARY EDITIONS / 1973

Library of Congress Cataloging in Publication Data

Garland, Henry Burnand.
  Lessing, the founder of modern German literature.

  "Fisrt published 1937."
  Bibliography: p.
  1. Lessing, Gotthold Ephraim, 1729-1781.
PT2406.G3 1973   838'.6'09   73-95
ISBN 0-8414-1375-4 (lib. bdg.)

Manufactured in the United States of America.

LESSING

The Founder of
Modern German Literature

by

H. B. GARLAND, M.A., Ph.D.

Professor of German in the
University College of the South West, Exeter

BOWES & BOWES
CAMBRIDGE
1949

First Published 1937
Second Impression 1949
All Rights Reserved

PRINTED IN GREAT BRITAIN BY JARROLD AND SONS LIMITED, NORWICH

PREFACE

THIS book is intended to supply the need for a recent English work on Lessing. It aims at presenting clearly and concisely the principal aspects of his work and activity. As much detail as possible on the subject of Lessing's own writings has been included ; but, for the sake of brevity, no complete account of the relationship of his ideas to particular thinkers has been attempted. The assessment of his indebtedness to Diderot, Shaftesbury and Harris seemed less important in such a book than a full statement of Lessing's own views.

In order that the various aspects of his work may be seen in their proper perspective, the book opens with an account of his life. It concludes with an attempt to determine not only his historical significance but also his permanent value.

Quotations are given in translation in the text and in German at the foot of the page. The letters PO. in the notes denote the edition of Lessing's works by Petersen and Olshausen, MK. the selected edition by Witkowsky in *Meyers Klassiker-Ausgaben*, familiar to students. The letters are quoted from the edition of Lachmann-Muncker.

In conclusion, the author would like to express his indebtedness to Mr. E. K. Bennett and to Dr. R. Samuel for valuable suggestions and criticism and to Mr. Geoffrey Grant, but for whom this book would not have been written.

October, 1937.   H.B.G.

TABLE OF CONTENTS

YOUNG LESSING

I. INTRODUCTORY

Louis XIV, the greatest representative of the divine right of monarchy, died in 1715. Some eighty years later the French Revolution had run its course, the mass had developed into a powerful political force and a new nationalistic spirit was fast emerging. The eighteenth century witnessed in fact the passing of one epoch and the birth of our own age.

The autocratic government by princes, continuing through the eighteenth century, though it had plainly outlived its political purpose, fostered an aristocratic art which found its finest expression in Germany in the music of Mozart and in the magnificent palaces built for the nobility by men such as Fischer von Erlach and Lukas von Hildebrandt. It was indeed almost impossible for music and architecture to dispense with princely aid, since only the very rich could maintain orchestras and singers or build themselves residences whose construction would afford scope to the architect.

But in literature aristocratic patronage played only a minor part. In Germany, as in England and France, the professional literary man emerged as a new type. The writer needed no material more expensive than his paper, pen and ink. And so Lesage appeared at the very beginning of the century as the first author to live on the receipts from the publication of his works. He was soon followed by others, of whom the most famous is perhaps our own Dr Johnson. In Germany, in the eighteenth century, the first and most famous exponent of literature as a career was Lessing. Other authors relied either upon academic employments or on private means for their maintenance, and these were sometimes, as with

Klopstock and Goethe, augmented by the generosity of enlightened patrons. Lessing alone of the important writers of the period depended solely on the industry of his pen from his adolescence till he was past forty years of age.

There were certainly many lesser men who sought to live by authorship and journalism, but the miserable financial gains, which this career afforded, tempted the majority into facile hack-work and destroyed in consequence their individuality and sincerity. Lessing, however, through all his difficulties and his distress preserved his personality intact. His formidable strength of character overcame all hindrances and, at this unpropitious date, gave to the world the spectacle of a completely independent man of letters. In a word, Lessing is the first modern figure in German literature.

2. CHILDHOOD AND SCHOOLDAYS

Gotthold Ephraim Lessing was born on 23rd January, 1729, in Kamenz, in what was then the Electorate of Saxony. This little town lies some thirty miles northeast of Dresden. Then as now it was no more than a quiet country town.[1] But the surroundings in which Lessing passed his boyhood left singularly little mark upon his personality. No description of its landscape or of the architectural peculiarities of the town throws any light upon his work. His was a cosmopolitan temperament, naturally at home in great cities, and Kamenz could only have appeared to him as a hindering and restricting environment, had he been obliged to remain there throughout his adolescence. Circumstances, however, early withdrew him from its influence, so that its effect upon him is negligible.

More important was the atmosphere of the family into which he was born. His father, Johann Gottfried Lessing (1693–1770), was a man of education but pos-

[1] Its population was just over 2,000 in the first half of the eighteenth century.

sessed of small means. In the eighteenth century, theology was the only accessible faculty for the poor student and Gottfried Lessing had in fact followed this course at the University of Wittenberg. His hope of an academic career was frustrated by the poverty of the family, so that in 1718 he returned to his native Kamenz as an assistant pastor. While still the equivalent of an English curate he married in 1725 Justina Salome Feller, an excellent practical housewife, who had no understanding for the intellectual interests and ambitions of her second son Gotthold. Eight years after the marriage the father was at last nominated principal pastor, but even then his income remained a very meagre one. His financial position was not improved by the rapid increase in the size of his family. Of twelve children five died in childhood (no unusual proportion in an age when the principles of domestic hygiene were but little understood), but the father was sorely taxed to maintain and educate the remaining seven on his slender income. It remains a matter for admiration and astonishment that he should have been able to send five of his sons to the university and even on occasion to pay their debts. This drain upon his resources was only checked at length by the borrowing of money, with the liabilities of which he was still encumbered at his death. Under such a burden it was not unnatural that his intellectual activities should gradually cease. Yet up to 1732 he had published several theological works of his own as well as translations of English and French books. His son, Gotthold, always esteemed and respected him highly, in spite of misunderstandings during the former's university career, and this relationship to his father is responsible for the sympathetic and comprehending attitude to orthodox Christianity, which he showed throughout his mature career, however much his own views might diverge from it.

From the father, too, came a precocious love of books. At the age of six Gotthold refused to be painted with a

bird-cage in his hand, but demanded instead a pile of
books.   His first schooling was in Kamenz, where he
received the foundations of his thorough classical education, for even the school-books were written in Latin.

The most important phase of his school-career was
now to follow.   In 1741 he was allotted a place and later
a scholarship in St Afra's School, Meissen.   The curriculum of this famous school, though restricted according
to modern conceptions, and its standard of teaching
were both on an unusually high level for the age.
Religious devotions occupied an important place, but the
principal feature of the curriculum was of course Latin.
Nevertheless religious instruction, Greek, French,
mathematics, history and geography received attention.
Music, drawing and Italian were among optional subjects.   Among the masters, Klimm, the mathematician,
had the greatest influence on Lessing, not in this study
alone, but by introducing him to modern German
literature (Hagedorn, Gleim, Haller) and by his more
practical and less pedantic attitude to learning.   The
pupils had no real holidays and this was another factor
which diminished the influence of Kamenz on Lessing.
Only twice did he visit his home for a brief stay between
1741 and 1746.   Lessing was not a model pupil, for he
already possessed an independent mind which saw the
weaknesses of his masters and also led him into studies
which lay outside the beaten track of the curriculum.
Alone, he read Homer, Anacreon, Plautus and Terence.
The school, however, in no way hindered his development,
and though his masters did not always approve of him,
they recognized in their reports the power of his mind.
By 1745 the sixteen-year-old Lessing felt that the school
had nothing more to give him; family circumstances
obliged him, however, to remain there for another year.
During this final year Lessing had his only experience of
the horrors of war, for Meissen was bombarded on
15th December, 1745, during the course of the Second
Silesian War.   This incident may well have contributed

to his subsequent aversion from war, for a letter of 1st February, 1746, gives a vivid description of the pitiable state of the town: "You rightly pity poor Meissen, which now looks more like a burial ground than the town it once was. In each house there are thirty to forty wounded men whom no one dare approach, for all those who are fairly seriously hit have the fever."[1] Lessing himself was spared from harm or sickness during this period. Four months later, in June 1746, he took his leave of St Afra's.

He had acquired a thorough knowledge of the classics, which was to stand him in good stead in an age when much valuable learning was still being embodied in Latin books and when the study of Greek antiquity was to undergo a striking revival. On the other hand he had been taught to regard book-learning as all-important. The years that followed were to bring a revolution in his outlook, but the positive gains of his schooling remained of permanent value to him.

3. THE PRODIGAL SON

Lessing matriculated at the University of Leipzig on 20th September, 1746. Leipzig, then known as " Little Paris," was not only the centre of fashion and of literary life in the first half of the eighteenth century, but was also enjoying a period of exceptional commercial prosperity.[2] This, combined with the opportunities for journalistic hack-work, naturally afforded in this centre of the publishing trade, made it a particularly suitable place of study for those poor students who had to eke out a scanty allowance with whatever tutoring and scribbling they could find. On the intellectual side, Leipzig was the centre of operations of Gottsched's literary party, whose prestige

[1] " Sie betauern mit Recht das arme Meisen, welches jezo mehr einer Toden Grube als der vorigen Stadt ähnlich siehet. Es liegen in denen meisten Häusern immer noch 30 bis 40 Verwundete, zu denen sich niemand sehre nahen darff, weil alle welche nur etwas gefährlich getroffen sind, das hizige Fieber haben."

[2] Its population was then about 26,000.

had however already been shaken outside Leipzig by the
attacks of the Swiss critics, Bodmer and Breitinger, and
inside by the disaffection of his former allies, the company
of actors led by Frau Neuber.

Lessing was designed to follow the paternal course, but
his attendance at the theological lectures very soon left
much to be desired. The lecturers who commanded his
respect were principally the philologist, Christ, and the
mathematician, Kästner. Both of these exercised a
considerable (in the case of Kästner personal) influence on
the young student, and he always mentioned them later
with respect. But lectures could not and did not occupy
the whole of his time. At first he devoted himself
exclusively to study, poring over his books in the third-
floor room which he shared with a fellow-student from
St Afra's. This seclusion could not, however, last for
ever in the gaiety and bustling activity of Leipzig. Lessing had not yet freed himself from the tradition of St
Afra's, had not yet realized that he was free to dispose of
his time as he might think fit. He was soon to make a
friend who would open his eyes to enjoyments and to
thoughts which so far had lain beyond his horizon.
This friend was Christlob Mylius, seven years older than
Lessing, with an experience of the world which could not
but excite the admiration of such a raw youth as Lessing
then was. Under his tutelage Lessing began to devote
himself to fencing and dancing. He mixed with
Mylius' friends, began to visit the theatre and soon
passed in the company of Mylius through the stage-door
to make the acquaintance of actors and actresses. He
took in hand the plan of a comedy, *The Young Scholar*,
dating from his Meissen days, and had the joy of seeing it
produced, in January 1748, by Frau Neuber's company.
News of this conduct soon reached Kamenz, and
it will be readily understood that Pastor Lessing
and his wife regarded it as reprehensible in the
extreme. Nor was their concern diminished by the fact
that Mylius was known to be a freethinker. The not un-

natural result was Lessing's recall home in January 1748.

There he remained three months, in the course of which he was able to reassure his parents as to his moral character and to gain a very important point, permission to abandon the theological career for the study of medicine. His good temper during this trying period is testified by an incident recorded by his brother Karl. Lessing's sister, uneducated and bigoted, had discovered love-poems (they were of course so-called Anacreontic poems addressed to Lauras and Corinnas who did not exist) and had promptly thrown them on the fire for the good of her brother's soul. Lessing remained quite unmoved by this incident and betrayed no ill-feeling whatsoever. The reconciliation completed, and his slight debts paid, he returned once more in the spring of 1748 to dangerous Leipzig.

It was in fact dangerous for him. Scarcely was he back in Leipzig than he relapsed into the old ways, renewed his contacts with the theatre and the actors, and devoted himself to writing comedies. Worse was to follow. The finances of the company failed and the actors left Leipzig. Lessing, always unpractical in money-matters, remained behind as the guarantor of their debts, an undertaking obviously far beyond his feeble resources. As might be expected, the debtors, once at a safe distance, left their guarantor in the lurch and Lessing had to face an impossible task alone.. For the first and only time in his life he was now guilty of a dishonourable action. As the creditors became more pressing, he saved himself by flight.

Lessing's intention was to make for Berlin, there to join Mylius. On the way, however, he fell ill in Wittenberg. When he recovered, he secured his father's permission to study at the University of Wittenberg and matriculated there in August 1748. But his dissatisfaction with academic life, the pressure of his creditors, from whom he had not escaped, and a praiseworthy desire for financial independence, drove him already in November

B

to leave Wittenberg for Berlin, there to make his living as best he could.

Lessing's literary work in Leipzig showed no trace of his future greatness. His play *Damon* is worthless, while *The Young Scholar*, in spite of its success on the stage, is in no way a characteristic work; the same may be said of *The Misogynist*, written at Wittenberg in 1748. Nevertheless his contacts with the stage had given him a valuable insight into the practical problems of the theatre. His poems, devoid of any vital experience, serve only to show that his ability lay in other fields. But the awakening of Lessing's literary interests was a step of the first importance, and in this the influence of the much abused, and often rightly abused, Mylius was undoubtedly beneficial. Mylius could only have done permanent harm to a weaker character than himself, and the determined and rapidly maturing Lessing soon showed a healthy independence.

The irritation which characterized the correspondence between Lessing and his parents at this time was inevitable. The various points in dispute are really incidental. The fundamental issue was this. The parents naturally wished him to qualify as soon as possible for a respectable and secure post. They would then be freed of one burden and would perhaps have secured from him welcome financial support in the education of the younger children. Lessing on the other hand was aware of his powers, was interested only in intellectual matters, cared little for a settled and secure post and abhorred everything which might cramp and obstruct his free development. This attitude was crystallized into a clear and conscious design in a letter to his mother, dated 20th February, 1749. Though assuring his parents of his love and gratitude, he is perfectly definite that he will neither return home nor to the university, but will live by his own endeavours. This mature and decisive letter marks the end of Lessing's youth.

4. HARD TIMES

Berlin, now the scene of Lessing's activities, was then a rapidly developing city, but its population was still under 100,000. Since the accession of Frederick the Great in 1740 it had become the acknowledged centre of free-thought in Germany. The most daring opinions in religious matters could there be expressed without fear of police action, though the latter were sharp enough in suppressing any unauthorized political allusions. Lessing later characterized this press freedom of Berlin in satirical terms—" It amounts simply and solely to freedom to offer as many stupid remarks against religion as one will."[1] Mylius (who had already established himself here in Berlin) over-estimated, however, the indulgence of the authorities and was soon in trouble over his journal, *The Soothsayer (Der Wahrsager).*

On Lessing's arrival in Berlin his state was a pitiable one. He had not even a decent suit in which to present himself to influential persons. At first he lived with Mylius and helped the latter in writing reviews for the *Berlinische priviligierte Zeitung.* Nine thalers (roughly 27s.) sent by the father to pay his journey home were spent instead on a new suit of clothes and Lessing began henceforth to feel himself at home in Berlin. But his circumstances were still difficult enough. He had still from time to time to ask for small advances from home. Some money came from the plays which he had written in Leipzig and Wittenberg. Others were now written (*The Old Maid*) and published. Translation, poorly paid as it was, constituted, however, his principal source of revenue.

In 1750, together with Mylius, he drew up the plan for an ambitious quarterly dealing with the theatre, *Contributions to the History and Encouragement of the Theatre.* This periodical marks a most important stage in Lessing's

---

[1] " Sie reducirt sich einzig und allein auf die Freyheit, gegen die Religion so viel Sottisen zu Markte zu bringen, als man will." Letter to Nicolai, 25th August, 1769.

development.   He now abandoned the hand-to-mouth
hack journalism of his first year in Berlin and turned his
hand to serious criticism ; and he now finally outgrew
the influence of Mylius, whose flippancy and inaccuracy
so angered Lessing that after the fourth number the
latter withdrew from the enterprise, which then immediately ceased.

Lessing had now shown himself to be a journalist of
merit and, when in December 1750 Mylius resigned his
post as reviewer to the *Berlinische priviligierte Zeitung*, it
was Lessing who took his place.   A secure if small
income was now assured, the immediate result of which
was an amelioration in the relations between Lessing and
his father.   In the letters from the end of 1750 onward,
there is a more amicable tone and they are accompanied
by copies of his new reviews, which shows that the father
had begun to take an interest in his son's literary career.
The Freethinker ("which the worthy theologians shall not
only read, but also praise," as Lessing wrote to his father
on 28th April, 1749), *The Jews* and *The Treasure* all belong
to this period, though they were not published until
later, but Lessing was soon to abandon the ambition to
become a " German Molière " and to devote himself
principally to criticism.

His progress in Berlin was, however, slow and at the
end of 1751 he returned to Wittenberg, there to resume
for a time his studies.   In April 1752 he graduated
Master of Arts, but it was only in the late autumn of that
year that he returned to Berlin.   Wittenberg had given
him a valuable opportunity to extend his reading, which
he now, at the age of twenty-three, prosecuted with
design as well as enthusiasm.   In this period fall his
studies of Horace as well as his discovery of a poem
of Andreas Scultetus.   Meanwhile an incident had
occurred in Berlin which, though trivial in itself, was to
have serious consequences later in Lessing's career.
Voltaire was, since July 1750, a much-lionized figure at
the court of Frederick the Great.   Through the influence

of Voltaire's secretary, Richier de Louvain, Lessing was commissioned to make translations of Voltaire's work, notably of his minor historical writings. Through the same intermediary, Lessing was able in December 1753 to obtain a copy of *Le Siècle de Louis XIV* before publication. Voltaire, on learning that the work was in unauthorized hands even before it was available to the Royal circle, demanded the immediate return of Lessing's copy. But Lessing had already left for Wittenberg with the book still in his possession. Voltaire leaped at once to the conclusion that Lessing intended to sponsor a pirated edition. An embittered correspondence ensued during the course of which Lessing returned the book to him. But incalculable harm had already been done, for Voltaire had complained to the King, who thus first heard the name of Lessing in very unfavourable circumstances, which he never forgot.

Once back in Berlin, in November 1752, Lessing resumed his journalistic activity. He continued his reviewing and added the finishing touches to works begun in Wittenberg. He was now a member of the Monday Club, a little group of eight intellectuals who met on one evening a week and discussed literature over their wine or beer. In this company Lessing met Ramler, the poet, and later Nicolai, then an ardent member of the advance guard of literature, however much he may have lagged behind later. A third friend, whom he met in 1753, was Moses Mendelssohn, a Jew of poor origin and upright mind, on whose character Lessing drew for the justification of the noble Jew in the play *The Jews*. These three were to remain lifelong friends of Lessing, and Mendelssohn in particular was of help to him in clarifying his philosophical ideas. Lessing was now no longer the poverty-stricken lonely youth who had come to Berlin in threadbare clothes. He was by no means well-off, but his name was known and his pen both respected and feared. Already he was preparing a collected edition of his works, of which the first two volumes appeared in duodecimo in 1753.

For nearly three years Lessing lived in Berlin a life outwardly uneventful, in close contact with his three friends. His literary activity in these years was considerable. The earlier *Contributions* were succeeded in 1754 by another periodical, the *Theatrical Library*, which was both more up-to-date and more thorough than its predecessor. He published in the same year an edition of selected works of the lately deceased Mylius, accompanied by a preface which was more honest than kind. For the first time he was involved in violent controversy, his opponent being Pastor Lange, the translator of Horace.[1] From this quarrel, the climax of which was the famous *Vademecum*, Lessing emerged with increased prestige. The rehabilitations of Cardanus, of the author of the *Ineptus Religiosus* and of Cochläus[2] further established his reputation as a scholar. Finally his tragedy, *Miss Sara Sampson*, was published in the spring of 1755 and successfully performed in July of that year. Yet notwithstanding his literary success and his satisfactory personal relationships in Berlin, Lessing suddenly left the city in October 1755 and established himself in Leipzig.

5. CHANGE OF SCENE

Lessing's motives for this sudden departure are not entirely clear. Possibly he felt that continued close association with his friends would hinder his own free development. Possibly he was simply weary of their company and course of life. This was not the only occasion on which he felt that a change of surroundings was a necessity for him. His correspondence with his friends betrays no irritation or misunderstanding. A clue may perhaps be found in his letter to G. A. von Breitenbauch of 12th December, 1755, in which he first mentions that he is working on his *Doctor Faust*. It is

---

[1] See below pp. 45–49.   [2] Published in *Schriften*. 3, *Teil*. 1754.

very probable that he had to separate himself from his friends in order to be able to devote himself to this project which had not their approval. This is borne out by a mildly sarcastic reference to this Faust play in a letter from Mendelssohn of 19th November, 1755.

The new play, however, did not advance very fast. Lessing, who had perforce abandoned his Berlin reviewing on his departure, now began to look round for a new source of revenue. His desire was to travel and his friend, Professor Sulzer, was already negotiating with a view to obtaining for him a post as travelling tutor. This project was, however, abandoned in December 1755, as Lessing had made contact in Leipzig with a wealthy young man named Winckler, with whom he was to travel to Holland, England, France and Italy. After many delays, they at last set out on 10th May, 1756. They had proceeded no further than Amsterdam when news reached them of the outbreak of hostilities between Austria and Prussia in August 1756. This was the beginning of the Seven Years' War. Winckler at once hastened to Leipzig; Lessing still accompanied him, for it was hoped that the campaign would be of brief duration and that the suspended journey might then be resumed. Lessing, although Saxon by birth, was Prussian in his sympathies; Berlin was his real home. Hence quarrels soon occurred on political questions with the Saxon Winckler, and these led to a complete rupture. Winkler refused to pay the indemnity of six hundred thalers (about £90) which had been stipulated in the agreement in the event of an abandonment of the journey, and so Lessing was obliged to have recourse to legal proceedings, which at first wasted his valuable time in Leipzig and then consumed the greater part of the sum in costs before he finally won the case in 1764.

His stay in Leipzig thus dragged on, but it was soon rendered agreeable by a new acquaintance. This newly-won friend was a major in the Prussian service, Ewald von Kleist (1715–59). Kleist was a poet of merit and a man of great personal qualities. Though he was now forty-two, while Lessing was only twenty-eight, a close personal friendship arose between the two, which surpassed in genuine affection any of Lessing's relationships with men. The news of his death from wounds at Riga called forth in Lessing expressions of the profoundest grief and dismay. And so this stay at Leipzig, which had been begun reluctantly on account of Winckler, was soon continued voluntarily for the sake of his new friend. Only in the early summer of 1758, on Kleist's departure for service elsewhere, did Lessing return to Berlin.

This stay in Leipzig had valuable influence on Lessing, very different from that of his first visit there as a student. His eyes had been opened to a new world. He had associated there with soldiers, and however much he disliked their profession, he had come to realize their worth as men. It was a more robust and manly Lessing who returned to the literary world of Berlin, with its intrigues and its back-biting. Though *Minna von Barnhelm* was only written five years later, after the death of Kleist, the character of von Tellheim is a monument to him and to his influence on Lessing.

CHAPTER II

THE ZENITH

1. THE CRITIC MILITANT

THE beneficial effects of the period of repose and of the deepening of Lessing's character in Leipzig were at once evident. He plunged into literary work with a vigour and an energy which surpassed even that of the earlier period in Berlin. In 1759 appeared his fables, accompanied by a theoretical treatise on the form, his patriotic tragedy *Philotas*, and the edition of Logau's epigrams. But the most important event of this year was the inauguration of the *Letters concerning the most recent Literature*. These letters, which appeared as a periodical at the rate of three to each weekly number, show indeed the influence of Lessing's contacts with his military friends. They constitute a campaign, conducted with skilful generalship and resolute aggressiveness, the objective of which was the purging of German literature of the mediocrities which encumbered it. Though Nicolai and Mendelssohn were collaborators from the first, by far the greater number of essays in the first two years were from Lessing's pen. While he led this campaign, the " *Literaturbriefe* " were the decisive arbiters in German literature. Only after Lessing's withdrawal did their influence and prestige decline.

The increased virulence of Lessing's criticism resulted entirely from his convictions as to the importance of German literature and from the genuine indignation he felt against those nonentities who obstructed its development. His personal character was in no way embittered and these few years in Berlin were in fact among the happiest in his life. He was popular in a circle of numerous friends and captivated his landlady by such unexpected charm that she remembered him in her will, though Lessing declined the bequest. His correspondence with Kleist's friend, the poet Gleim, author of *War Songs of a Grenadier*, for which Lessing wrote a laudatory preface, bears witness to his good-humour at the time, whilst numerous anecdotes portray him as an excellent companion at the drinking parties at the " Baumannshöhle."

In spite of his absorption in literary work (he was now engaged on his *Life of Sophocles*), Lessing realized that his inability to obtain the favour of the King placed a bar before his advancement to any official position. In 1760 his candidature for the membership of the Academy was rejected. His financial position left much to be desired, as is proved by the fact that in August 1758 he received a welcome and tactful present of 100 thalers (about £15) from Kleist. His thoughts already hovered round the possibility of obtaining some secure and remunerative post. Yet he was unwilling to take any decisive step, as a letter to his father of 3rd April, 1760, shows : " As long as I can live by my work, and live fairly comfortably, I have not the slightest wish to become the slave of an office. If I am offered one, then I will accept it ; but to take the slightest step to obtain one, even though I may not be exactly too conscientious, I am at any rate too easy-going and indolent." The amenities of Berlin were not improved by the occupation of the city by the Austrians and Russians in October, and it therefore comes as no great surprise that Lessing actually accepted a position as secretary to General Tauentzien and left Berlin suddenly and without the knowledge of his friends on 7th November, 1760.

2. THE MADDING CROWD

Lessing's flight from Berlin—for flight it was— signified an entirely new departure in his life. The chief motive seems to have been financial, to which may be added a weariness with his Berlin mode of life, which had become void to him, and a desire to take part for once in practical life. His letters show that he was far from happy over his sudden decision. " You will perhaps wonder at my decision," he wrote to Ramler on 6th December, 1760. " To tell the truth there is at least a quarter of an hour every day when I wonder at it myself."[1] To Mendelssohn he is even more explicit: " Remorse at having undertaken so entire a change in my mode of life with the mere intention of making my so-called fortune, will not fail to appear."[2] Yet he continued in this post for nearly five years, so that Breslau cannot have remained so uncongenial as these letters from his first days there would suggest. It is nevertheless clear from letters to Ramler (6th December, 1760) and to his father (30th November, 1763) that he had no intention of remaining permanently in the general's employment. In the last-mentioned letter he gave as his reasons for accepting, the need for the restoration of his health, for rest and for money, which he typically devoted chiefly to acquiring an excellent library.[3]

His duties in Breslau were light. He rose late (sometimes not before ten) and was yet able to complete his task during the morning. He had chiefly to concern himself with correspondence regarding the commissariat service and the exchange of prisoners. He was even able to devote a certain amount of time to his own studies and at the same time to visit the theatre assiduously and to play cards in the officers' casino. He was at this time a passionate gambler and often played for high stakes, in spite of warnings from all sides, but does not seem on the whole to have had any serious losses.

Lessing himself confessed that domestic economy was not his strong point.[4] His salary in Breslau was excellent

[1] " Sie werden sich vielleicht über meinen Entschluss wundern. Die Wahrheit zu gestehen, ich habe jeden Tag wenigstens eine Viertelstunde, wo ich mich selbst darüber wundere."

[2] " Die Reue wird ohnedem nicht aussenbleiben, eine so gänzliche Veränderung meiner Lebensart in der blossen Absicht, mein sogenanntes Glück zu machen, vorgenommen zu haben." 7th December, 1760.

[3] In 1768 his library numbered more than 6,000 volumes.

[4] Letter to Ramler, 7th September, 1761.

and on more than one occasion he was able to send not inconsiderable sums of money to various members of his family. This generosity however, coupled with his enormous expenditure on books, prevented him from saving more than a very small sum. In these circumstances it says much for his honesty that he refrained from making any speculative use of early information of the inflation of currency projected by Frederick the Great. His employer, General Tauentzien, is said to have made 150,000 thalers (say £22,500) by this means, but Lessing's integrity in this matter was exemplary and will earn him the general approval of a later age.

In spite of all other occupations Lessing's mind remained far from idle. Not only did he write *Minna von Barnhelm*, but it was in these years that he began archæological studies, to which he was stimulated by the work of Winckelmann; these were presently to culminate in *Laocoon*. Yet his dissatisfaction increased. In May 1762 he had written to Ramler, " I am tired of my present situation as I have never been tired of any previous one."[1] This longing for freedom appears again in letters written in 1763. It may well have been increased by a brief visit with the general to Potsdam, in the course of which he saw all his old Berlin friends. In any case, his unrest is expressed afresh after his return and again in 1764. He was now firmly determined to leave the general's service and after recovering from a serious bout of fever in the summer of 1764, he waited only for the conclusion of his protracted law-suit with Winckler to hand in his resignation. In October the news of the favourable verdict of the court reached him. A delay ensued however, occasioned by the illness of General Tauentzien. At last, in April 1765, he left Breslau and journeyed to Kamenz to pay his first visit to his home since 1756. A month later he returned to Berlin.

---

[1] " Ich bin meiner jetzigen Situation so überdrussig, als ich noch einer in der Welt gewesen bin." 30th May, 1762.

3. New Enterprise

Lessing's intention before leaving Breslau had been to make use of his regained liberty in travelling. He is reported by Klose to have planned a journey to Greece. His visit to Berlin in May 1765 was therefore intended only to be a temporary one. And yet there was a secret hope in his mind that he might only be exchanging one secure position for another, for the death of de la Croze in February 1765 had left the post of Royal Librarian in Berlin vacant. Such a position was the height of Lessing's ambition, for it would have enabled him to combine financial security and ability to assist his family with greatly increased opportunities for study and literary work.

And so it was with an eye to this appointment that he hastened the completion of *Laocoon*, which he had already prepared in Breslau, and which finally appeared at Easter 1766. But Lessing's hopes and the efforts of his influential friends were vain. Frederick remembered only the unfortunate skirmish with Voltaire, possibly also the association with the suspect Mylius, and curtly rejected his candidature. Hope flickered again for a moment, when Winckelmann withdrew his acceptance on the ground of inadequate remuneration, but the King remained adamant against Lessing, and appointed a Frenchman to the post. It is curiously ironical that, through carelessness in first names, an insignificant Benedictine, Antoine Pernéty, received the office which the King had intended for Jacques Pernéty.

During the later stages of these negotiations, Lessing undertook a journey to Pyrmont, acting as companion to a young man. This expedition was presumably a welcome distraction from the wearisome wait for news of the post of Librarian. On his return in October 1766 to Berlin by way of Göttingen, Cassel and Halberstadt, where he once more visited Gleim, Lessing found that another had finally been appointed. The growing dissatisfaction with his previous mode of life became more acute, when, in addition to his disappointment over the library appointment, his health began to suffer from the sedentary nature of his occupation. It was therefore a welcome surprise to him when in November 1766 he received the first tentative inquiry as to his willingness to accept a post differing entirely from anything he had yet undertaken.

Hamburg, the centre of prosperous trade and of a well-to-do middle class, had possessed a permanent theatre since 1763. In 1766 the attempt was made to establish in addition a permanent repertory company. The actors were to be guaranteed pensions on retirement, an annual prize was proposed for the best German play, and a salaried dramatist was to be attached to the theatre. This was the first endeavour to found a national theatre in Germany.

It was the position of dramatist and consultant to this theatre which was now offered to Lessing.[1] Nothing could have been more welcome to him. His financial difficulties were acute, so that the proposed income of 3,200 marks (about £160, naturally worth more then than now) promised to extricate him from an awkward position. He was weary of Berlin after the disappointment of his hopes and looked forward to the change of scene to Hamburg. And he was moved to enthusiasm at the thought that he would be able to assist the rise of a German national theatre. On 10th January, 1767, he signed the contract with a feeling of immense relief that he was for ever turning his back on Berlin,[2] and his departure actually took place in the following April.

On the 22nd April, 1767, the theatre was opened and on the same day Lessing published the programme of his periodical, *The Hamburg Dramaturgy*, by which he intended to maintain the interest of the public in the theatre. His

---

[1] Lessing declined the first proposition, which was that he should become house-dramatist, and accepted a compromise by which he was not bound to deliver plays at any stated time.

[2] Letter to Gleim, 1st February, 1767.

personal hopes from this enterprise were high. His dramatic works were to be finished and produced ; and he reckoned on " a calm and pleasant life for several years to come."[1]   But in these as in the prospects of the theatre itself he was to be woefully disappointed.   Intrigues and cabals among the actors destroyed the unity of the troupe and diminished Lessing's influence.   He had no control over the choice of plays, so that his advocacy of Shakespeare was confined to the pages of *The Hamburg Dramaturgy*.   The interest of the public was lukewarm.   In the winter of 1767–8 the company went to Hanover, as their finances would not allow them to hold out in Hamburg at a time when Advent and Lent meant serious interruptions of the performances.

Lessing had by now embarked upon his only financial enterprise.   Shortly after his arrival in Hamburg he had entered into partnership with J. J. C. Bode, who had just founded a combined publishing and printing business.   Such savings as Lessing still possessed after settling his Berlin debts, he sank in this enterprise which, however, brought him nothing but fresh liabilities. Within a very few months therefore he found the actuality of his Hamburg life very different from that depicted by his hopes.   The theatre was ailing and his business was but little better.

In the course of the summer of 1768 it became clear that the theatre was nearing its end.   The attendance decreased still further, its financial straits became more desperate.   Lessing resigned and shortly afterwards dissolved partnership with Bode.   *The Hamburg Dramaturgy*, which had already lagged behind in August 1767, still remained to be completed.   Not till the spring of 1769 did the last twenty numbers appear, in which Lessing's bitter disappointment at the failure of the enterprise expressed itself.   His financial situation was already precarious enough, and it was now further menaced by the threat of a pirated edition of *The Hamburg*

---

[1] Letter to Gleim, 1st February, 1767.

Dramaturgy. This danger stimulated Lessing in the Epilogue to a fierce and bitter exposure of his rivals.

In spite, however, of all disappointments and difficulties, Lessing's years in Hamburg were by no means unhappy. He soon had a circle of friends, before all others the Königs. As in Berlin during the Seven Years' War, he was known for his sociability. But he was nevertheless determined to leave Hamburg, once *The Hamburg Dramaturgy* was completed. The plan which he now conceived arose out of the studies which underlay *Laocoon.* On the 24th September, 1768, he wrote to his brother Karl that he intended to go to Rome. He ardently desired to study at first-hand the antiquities which had occupied his attention for some years, and in addition he had become very weary of a controversy in which he had been engaged since February 1768.

His opponent on this occasion was the antiquarian Klotz of Halle who, after unsuccessful flattering advances to Lessing, had become his bitterest adversary and lost no opportunity of attacking *Laocoon.* Klotz, like Pastor Lange fourteen years earlier, was unable to dissociate the opinions from the personal character of his adversary, and a literary war ensued which continually increased in ferocity. For Lessing the fruits of this dispute were the *Letters of Antiquarian Content* (1768–9) and the essay, *How the Ancients portrayed Death* (1769). But though Lessing's refutation of Klotz was complete, he could not quell his noisy adversary. He was somewhat annoyed with himself that he had not accepted the advice of his friends (notably Mendelssohn) who had counselled him to ignore the onslaughts of Klotz. ·And so it was with the longing to escape from this petty atmosphere that he planned to leave Germany for Italy in the spring of 1769.

The settlement of his affairs in Hamburg took, however, longer than he had anticipated. His debts were considerable and he was obliged to sell the remainder of his library, part of which had already been disposed of in order to settle his debts in Berlin. The months dragged on in Hamburg and he seemed no nearer his departure. Offers of a post connected with the theatre came from Vienna, but after a brief period of reflection he rejected these. On the 10th August, 1769, he wrote to Nicolai that he was still firmly resolved on the Italian journey.

Shortly afterwards in September, however, Lessing's Brunswick friend, Ebert, sent to him a proposition which made Lessing pause. This was the offer of the position of Librarian at the Ducal Library in Wolfenbüttel. It proceeded from the heir to the Duchy of Brunswick, a man of intellectual interests. The post of librarian had always had attractions for Lessing and the Library of Wolfenbüttel was, he knew, an excellent one. He had indeed already visited it in 1756, when on the way to Hamburg in the company of Winckler. Further, he was promised that the Italian journey should only be postponed and that after he had explored the resources and put in order the treasures of the library, he would be free to travel. He had therefore little hesitation in accepting the post. A visit to the Court of Brunswick terminated to the satisfaction of all parties, and Lessing was to take up his duties as soon as he had brought his affairs in Hamburg to a conclusion. Lessing at first intended to leave for Wolfenbüttel in November 1769. But the settlement of his debts proved a more difficult and protracted business than he had anticipated, all the more so as the auctions of his books did not realize anything like the sum on which he had reckoned. In December, moreover, news reached Frau Eva König, the wife of Lessing's friend, that her husband had died in Venice. Before his departure König had recommended his family to Lessing's care and the latter was in consequence doubly loth to quit Hamburg immediately. And so the spring came ; Lessing fell ill, recovered, delayed his departure still longer in order to spend a few days with Herder, who was then bound for France, and whose *Critical Woods*, arising out of *Laocoon*, had won Lessing's respect, and finally arrived in Wolfenbüttel on 4th May, 1770.

c

CHAPTER III

THE LIBRARIAN

1. THE LIBRARY REVIVES

LESSING came to Wolfenbüttel full of enthusiasm. The Library was a noted one and he promised himself that its treasures would afford the solution of many questions which had excited his interest, but which had remained in abeyance through lack of facilities for research. His material position was modest but secure. His salary was 600 thalers (about £90) with free residence and firing in the old Palace which housed the Library. With this sum he was able gradually to settle outstanding debts and even on occasion to help his father and, after the latter's death, the remainder of the family; for he never ceased to realize his indebtedness to his parents.

His duties involved the putting in order of the books and manuscripts and a revision of the catalogue, besides which he had to attend to the numerous inquiries from scholars for information or for the loan of works. In his relationship to his correspondents he was generally a model librarian. He was always willing to search through books and manuscripts in quest of some forgotten work, to lend works and in every way to make the Library as great a force in the furtherance of learning as was in his power. He had time too for research of his own. The first year brought an important work in the rehabilitation of Berengar of Tours. And in the Contributions *To History and Literature*, which appeared from 1773 onwards, he proved himself one of the foremost scholars of his time.

Wolfenbüttel was a small and decayed town of about 6,000 inhabitants. It had suffered particularly by the transference of the Ducal residence to Brunswick in 1754. Many of the buildings were ruinous and even those housing the library were crumbling in Lessing's day. Lessing's life was necessarily a solitary one, for all social activity had migrated with the Court to Brunswick, about eight miles away. Lessing, however, was in the first months too busy exploring the resources of the library to suffer from his isolation. After a fortnight he wrote to Nicolai (17th May, 1770) expressing his satisfaction, in spite of the enormous contrast to his life in Hamburg. A cordial correspondence began in June with Eva König, the widow of his Hamburg friend, a correspondence which continued throughout the journey to Vienna, which the sad plight of her deceased husband's affairs compelled her to undertake in the autumn of 1770 and which lasted till the spring of the following year.

As the months passed, however, Lessing, who had been accustomed for so many years to active social intercourse and a circle of friends, began to find his isolation irksome. A tone of longing appears in the letters to Eva König. Lessing, who for so many years had troubled himself little about the company of women and who counted himself a confirmed bachelor,[1] began to yearn for a household of his own and for the company and solicitude of a loving wife. And so the correspondence with Eva gradually assumed a more intimate tone. His financial position, in view of the heavy drain imposed by the settlement of his debts and the assistance he gave to his family, would not permit of his marrying, and so he dabbled in the Hamburg lottery with small sums in their joint name, always with the remote hope that a sudden stroke of fortune would cut the financial tangle which forbade their union.

In September 1770 Lessing received the news of his father's death. In spite of all misunderstandings and complaints Lessing's relations with him had remained loyal and cordial, and so the tidings heightened the feeling of loneliness of which he was already aware. Its effect was to draw him more closely to Eva, though at the same time it augmented his difficulties, as he at once offered to

[1] Letter to Nicolai from Breslau, 22nd October, 1762.

take upon himself the settlement of the father's debts, incurred in helping the sons.

A momentary interruption of the desolate monotony of Lessing's life occurred in October, when his old friend Moses Mendelssohn paid a visit to Brunswick, but the correspondence with Eva König was in the long run the only really happy aspect of his life in Wolfenbüttel. In April 1771 he saw her for the first time in eight months, as she passed through Brunswick on her return from Vienna. This brief meeting—for she was eager to rejoin her two children in Hamburg as early as possible—drew them closer together, for Lessing now changed the address of his letters from " My dearest Madam " to " My dearest Friend," which in turn yielded in October to " My dear One " ; for in August he had paid a visit to Hamburg and there had become affianced to Eva, now thirty-five years old.

The enforced solitude of the Library now became less and less congenial to him, and he began to betray a weariness with life, which was new to him.[1] In February 1772, Eva had left Hamburg again for Vienna where she was to remain three years, and the great distance, which prevented any possibility of occasional visits, increased Lessing's loneliness and depression. These years were among the gloomiest of his whole life. Even the correspondence with Eva flagged on his side. In occasional ill-health (in 1771 he had been ill for six months on end) he laboured away at his learned writings, prepared a new edition of his youthful works and finished the old project of *Emilia Galotti*. A promise of advancement at the Brunswick Court gave a momentary ray of hope, only to be dropped without explanation, leaving Lessing in even greater bitterness of soul than before. His circumstances now became worse. He had even to borrow money and the family at Kamenz had at last to do without his assistance. His work no longer satisfied him, his dependence on the princely favour

---

[1] Letter to Eva, 27th June, 1772.

infuriated him and his solitude was now intolerable. And so after five long years he sought and obtained leave of absence to breathe for a space another and more congenial air.

2. Ironical Fulfilment

Lessing left Wolfenbüttel on 9th February, 1775. His first objective was Berlin, which he reached after spending a week at Leipzig *en route*. His brother Karl was in Berlin and the two passed a brief period together which did something to calm Lessing's nerves. In the second week of March he set out for Vienna, there to join Eva who had just completed the liquidation of her resources. His route southward lay through Dresden and Prague, and after many adventures on the bad Prussian roads he finally reached his goal on the 31st March, 1775. His original leave was exceeded and from Dresden he had petitioned for an extension.

In Vienna Lessing was most cordially received. Maria Theresa received him in audience, whilst *Minna von Barnhelm* and *Emilia Galotti* were performed in his honour. Such public distinctions had however but little charm for Lessing now and his one happiness was to be together with Eva once more. But the horizon did not long remain unclouded. Prince Leopold of Brunswick, the second son of the reigning Duke, had planned a journey to Italy, on which Lessing was to be his cicerone. It is possible that the Prince and his father imagined that this project would give pleasure to Lessing, whose earlier intention of going to Italy was known in Brunswick. Yet nothing could have been more unwelcome to Lessing than the appearance of the Prince in April in Vienna. In a few days he had to take his leave of Eva and set out on 25th April with the Prince and his tutor, von Warnstedt. Shortly afterwards Eva left Vienna for Hamburg by way of her native town of Heidelberg.

The Italian journey was not only unwelcome because it

deprived Lessing of the company of Eva.   He chafed
because he was not at liberty to follow his own itinerary,
but depended on the Prince who wandered aimlessly
hither and thither.   Moreover, he had had no opportunity to prepare himself by reading and study for the
journey, which was thus bound to be far less profitable
to him than it might have been in more favourable
circumstances.   Lessing's hopes were thus at last fulfilled, but in a way that could bring nothing but disappointment and irritation at wasted opportunities.

The party went first to Salzburg, and from there via
Brescia to Milan, and here on 8th May, 1775, his complaints begin.   Social duties absorbed too much of his
time and the heat and dust affected his eyes, which were
tired with excessive reading over a long period.   From
Milan they journeyed east to Venice, where Lessing
visited the grave of Eva's late husband, his friend König.
Then south to Florence, on to Leghorn, across the sea to
Corsica, back to the mainland at Genoa, then to Turin.
So they passed from point to point with much time
wasted in travelling.   In Turin late in August Lessing
began his Italian diary.   But little of personal interest is
to be found in it.   It is devoted chiefly to notes on books
to be read, on libraries, on the achievements of Italian
scholars and so on.   Lessing was never egocentric and
was attentive rather to objects and events around him
than to personal reactions and reflections.

From Turin they passed through Pavia, Piacenza and
Modena, then once more southward, this time to Rome.
Neither the architectural beauties of Rome nor later the
situation of Naples roused his interest.   The enforced
journey told heavily on his spirits which were still further
depressed by Eva's apparent silence, for friends in Vienna
had failed to forward her letters to Lessing.   In Rome he
was received in audience by the Pope in his capacity as
cicerone to the Prince, but no trace of this visit occurs in
his letters or writings.   In Naples the Prince received
news that he had been nominated colonel-in-chief of a

Prussian regiment and hastened at once to join his new command. Lessing was thus at last delivered from this unproductive fulfilment of his old yearning. The party travelled together as far as Munich, where Lessing left his companions to proceed to Vienna, which he reached in December 1775. Here at last he obtained news of Eva.

In Dresden Lessing was received graciously by the Elector, with the hint of a future appointment, should he wish it. From there he passed to Kamenz for the last time. After a brief stay in Berlin he returned to Brunswick on 23rd February, 1776, after an absence of just over a year.

3. BRIEF HAPPINESS

Lessing returned to his duties with the firm determination to secure better financial conditions, which would enable him to marry, or else to leave the Duke's service. The threat of departure had the desired effect. His salary was raised and he was granted a new residence with 200 thalers bonus; he was also accorded a substantial loan for the payment of his debts, and further received the title Hofrat. This was an appreciable improvement in his position and accordingly, when the negotiations were completed in July 1776, he began to press on the preparations for his wedding, which was to take place in October.

Meanwhile recognition came from another quarter. Lessing was offered membership of the Academy of Mannheim, with an annual pension of 100 *louisdors* (about £75). He was also requested to assist the Mannheim theatre in an advisory capacity. This proposal was gladly accepted in September 1776. No obstacle whatever now stood in the way of the marriage. And so on 8th October, 1776, Lessing and Eva were at last quietly wedded in York near Hamburg. The couple returned at once to Wolfenbüttel, where Lessing's brief period of married happiness began. The letters of guests and of scholars visiting the library testify to the excellent understanding between Lessing and his wife and to their hospitality.

An interruption came on 17th January, 1777. Lessing left for Mannheim to fulfil his engagements there. It then transpired that the real intention in Mannheim had been to secure Lessing as director of the new theatre. This was entirely contrary to his own wishes and designs, as he had renounced all activity in connection with the theatre after the Hamburg fiasco and was now, moreover, perfectly happy in Wolfenbüttel. The irritation which this misunderstanding produced resulted in the cancellation of the pension granted him a few months before and Lessing returned to Wolfenbüttel. His domestic happiness was, however, more than sufficient consolation for this fresh experience of the inconstancy of princely favour.

In March 1777 Lessing's mother died, but his grief, though sincere, was not profound, for his relations with her had never been on the same cordial footing as those with his father. All through the summer Lessing and his wife lived on happily in Wolfenbüttel. In November 1777 they received a visit from Lessing's old friend, Moses Mendelssohn. The letter which Mendelssohn wrote to Lessing before his arrival reveals the change which domestic happiness had wrought in Lessing: " You seem to be in a calm and contented state, which harmonizes infinitely better with my manner of thinking, than that witty but somewhat bitter mood, which I thought I detected in you a few years ago."

But lasting happiness was always to be denied to Lessing. On 24th December his wife gave birth to a child which died within twenty-four hours. The mother lay unconscious for ten days ; on 5th January Lessing wrote to his brother Karl that he believed she had taken a turn for the better. His hope, however, was deceived and on 10th January, 1778, Eva Lessing died.

4. The Theological Feud

Lessing now stood alone, in bitterness of soul, to bear
the brunt of the fiercest conflict in which he had yet been
engaged. Already during Eva's lifetime, in 1777 he had
begun to publish in the Contributions to *History and
Literature* a series of fragments from the manuscript of
Reimarus' *Apologia for the reasonable Worshippers of God.*
This publication had called forth a storm of vehement
protest from the orthodox Protestant camp. Lessing
now took up the cudgels on behalf of the anonymous
author (for circumstances did not permit him to use
Reimarus' name) and throughout the early months of
1778 the eleven *Anti-Goeze* pamphlets flowed from his
vitriolic pen. Their virulence is partly explained by his
championship of the cause of tolerance, but certainly in
part also by the bitter despair into which the death of his
wife had plunged him. Brooding in his solitude over
the happiness which was denied to him, he had no other
occupation but this ruthless war of words, by which he
was able to give vent to the vain wrath which oppressed
him.

But this outlet was not available for long. The
orthodox party, finding that they could not silence Lessing in public controversy, had recourse to other means.
At the request of the ecclesiastical authorities the Duke
forbade Lessing in July 1778 to publish work until it had
been approved by the censorship in Brunswick. On
Lessing's request for a more exact statement of the position, the edict was made even stricter. It applied not
only to work printed and published in Brunswick but was
in fact general. Lessing's immediate impulse was to
resign his appointment in Wolfenbüttel, but his friends
persuaded him to abstain from this extreme measure.
And so he remained in Wolfenbüttel, in isolation not only
there but in the whole of Germany, forbidden to reply to
the attacks made upon him. The one activity which had
distracted him during the first months of his bereavement

was now denied, and he relapsed as the summer wore on into a state of gloomy depression, deeper than anything he had yet experienced.

The lowest ebb of Lessing's spirits at this period was reached in a letter written on 9th August, 1778, to Elise Reimarus, an old Hamburg friend and the daughter of the Reimarus whose manuscript had occasioned the storm of controversy.   In this letter he returns once more to the project of resignation and expresses his intention to " let the boat drift, whither the wind and the waves will."[1] But in the night of 10th August an idea struck him which was to be his salvation from this apathetic state of mind. He recalled an old dramatic project, which would give him an opportunity to present his views in an uncontroversial form.   From this inspiration came *Nathan the Wise*, at which Lessing worked throughout the winter. In the spring of 1779 the play was published and received everywhere with the most favourable judgments.   The writing of this work was of the greatest psychological value for Lessing, for it provided him with a vehicle for the many conflicting emotions which pressed upon his heart, and which would have destroyed him if they had not found expression here.

In September 1778 Lessing had paid a visit of a few weeks to Hamburg, which proved of some benefit to his health.   Since 1777 he had become increasingly subject to fits of drowsiness, which gradually became serious and embarrassing interruptions to his work and social life. But soon after his return from Hamburg the attacks recommenced and in the summer of 1779 he had also to reckon with serious bouts of fever.   Presently his sight began to fail too, and the rapid deterioration in his condition soon made it evident that his forces were failing. By the summer of 1780 he was unable to carry out unaided his duties as Librarian and he received an assistant, E. T. Langer.

His literary activity was now practically at an end, as

---

[1] "lasse den Kahn gehen, wie Wind und Wellen wollen."

continued concentration became impossible.   He paid a
visit to Gleim at Halberstadt and shortly afterwards, in
October 1780, once more spent a few weeks in Hamburg.
In Wolfenbüttel his only solace was the company of his
stepdaughter, Amalie König, now sixteen years of age.
All who saw Lessing at this time were aghast at the decay
of his powers.   He would sit silent and apparently asleep
for long periods in his chair, and it was clear to all that he
was failing rapidly.

Back in Wolfenbüttel he began already to consider his
death imminent.   He still found some pleasure in the
correspondence with Elise Reimarus, but the weakness of
his eyes made even this difficult.   At the beginning of
February he was still active enough to dine with the Duke
and with the Dowager Duchess, but on the evening of
3rd February, 1781, he had a stroke.   Twelve days later,
on 15th February, 1781, Lessing died at the early age of
fifty-two, worn out with his long struggle and the consequent strain on his constitution.

Part Four

LESSING AND RELIGION

CHAPTER IV

THE CRITIC OF CONTEMPORARY LITERATURE

I. THE STATE OF GERMAN LITERATURE IN 1750

ALL students of German literature are familiar with the fact that the dawn of the eighteenth century found Germany, in sharp contrast to England and France, without a literary tradition. Though this was long attributed exclusively to the protracted slaughter and destruction of the Thirty Years' War with its consequent lowering of cultural values, it seems probable that this was only the last of many factors (geographical, economic and social) which produced a decline in literature and the arts, already in evidence before the war broke out. Among these causes the most conspicuous were the geographical barriers to political unity in an age of poor communications, the shifting of trade from the overland route to the sea, with consequent benefit to the Western maritime nations at the expense of Germany, and the Reformation which produced more acute dissension and strife in Germany than elsewhere. The effect of these factors was of course reinforced and accelerated by the Thirty Years' War.

It has often been remarked that literary movements in Germany proceed generally from theoretical rather than practical beginnings, and so it was at the beginning of the eighteenth century. The first serious attempt to found a German literary tradition was the work of J. C. Gottsched (1700–66). His plan had the merit of simplicity. He proposed to create a German literature by straightforward imitation of French classical literature. Quite apart from considerations of national temperament and modes of thought and feeling, it is clear that the fundamental condition of French literature of the eighteenth century, a single central court,[1] was absent in Germany

[1] In any case the Courts, in so far as they had cultural interests, were under French influence. Even Frederick the Great wrote in French and ignored the new German literature.

39

and that the attempt could not but fail. Moreover, in addition to this error of judgment, Gottsched was quite unsuited to the task of raising the standard of German literature. His *Ars Poetica*[1] is astonishing in the crudity of its conception of literary creation. It is not, therefore, surprising that his authority was seriously menaced within a decade by the Swiss theorists, Bodmer and Breitinger,[2] whose desire to claim the wonders of religion as a subject matter for literature led them to set up an English poet as a model. This was Milton. Gottsched's success up to this point may be ascribed chiefly to his favourable position in Leipzig, the centre of the publishing trade of Germany, and to his resolute propagandist activities. Though the repute of the Swiss rapidly rose at Gottsched's expense, it cannot be said that their merits are much more than relative. They show scarcely any more understanding of poetic processes than Gottsched had exhibited. The dispute between these rival authorities continued for many years with increasing acrimony on Gottsched's part as it became more and more evident that he was fighting a losing battle.

By 1750, however, the creative activities of German writers began to be of importance and the sterile theoretical disputes no longer constituted the only feature of literary life. Haller's famous poem, *The Alps*, had already been in print for eighteen years. The *Fables* of Hagedorn had appeared in 1738; Gellert's novel, *The Swedish Countess*, was published in 1747–8 and his *Fables* in 1746 and 1748. All these, however, were eclipsed by the publication of the first three cantos of Klopstock's religious epic, *The Messiah*, in 1748. This meant fulfilment for the Swiss and disaster for Gottsched. A general reawakening had begun and one poet of power had appeared. However, the standard must not be exaggerated. None of these poets is now as readable as Pope or

---

[1] *Kritische Dichtkunst*, 1730.

[2] J. Bodmer (1698–1783), J. J. Breitinger (1701–76).

Thomson, while Gellert's novel is far below Richardson, not to speak of Fielding.

The works hitherto mentioned were of course the most advanced books of their time. The market was at the same time inundated with imitations and translations of French and to a lesser extent of English works. Such was the state of German literature when the nineteen-year-old Lessing, soon to be the foremost critic of the age, arrived in Berlin.

2. LESSING AS REVIEWER

It is not the least of Lessing's virtues that he was vitally interested in and preoccupied with the literature of his own day. And so, after a year of poverty and an abortive attempt at periodical literature,[1] he began his career, as many another young man has done, as a reviewer. Mylius, whatever his faults, was of positive assistance in obtaining for him this appointment on the staff of Voss' *Berlinische priviligierte Staats- und Gelehrten-Zeitung*. Week in, week out, Lessing wrote accounts and criticisms of literary productions of the most varied kinds, ranging from novelty packs of cards and collections of ghost stories and domestic hints, through every variety of poem and novel, to learned treatises on science, philosophy and religion.

He must often have found his task irksome, though its magnitude presented little difficulty to so voracious a reader. And indeed it had its rewards, for among the trash he was obliged to peruse, he necessarily stumbled from time to time upon works of the greatest interest, to which his slender purse would have denied him access, had he not, as a reviewer, received a free copy.

For four years (except for the months spent in Wittenberg in 1752) Lessing continued to write these criticisms. They show a rapidly increasing maturity in his opinions and in his incisive style. But their greatest benefit for

[1] *Beyträge zur Historie und Aufnahme des Theaters.* See below, p. 53

him was the necessity they imposed of formulating a
concise judgment in a minimum of time. They are
often no more than hastily executed hack-work, but they
are at all events clear and definite. They were the dis-
cipline which Lessing needed to develop his finest
qualities.

Other features of his mind appeared in these criticisms
—first and foremost his practical common-sense. Lessing is never an extremist; his moderation is the outcome,
not of timidity, but of a sensible, practical mind. So, in
the violent controversy over the value of rhyme in German poetry, he steered a course between those partisans
who declared it essential, and the opposing school who
would have abolished it. Rhyme was, in Lessing's
view, neither indispensable nor reprehensible. The poet
might adopt or discard it as he saw fit, and Lessing's
theatrical experience in Leipzig led him to add, with
justice, that it could be of great value to the actor as an
aid to memory.[1] These reasonable conclusions were
certainly not profoundly original, but they demonstrate
the sound sense of the man, who, at twenty-two, amid the
dust and heat of acrimonious literary controversy, could
ignore the clamour and arouse the animosity of both
parties.

Lessing was as yet no enemy to French taste and
literature, but he already had a lively appreciation of
English writers. Richardson and Fielding won his
unstinted praise. His acceptance of foreign work was,
however, not uncritical, as an attack on the fashionable
adulation of English work proves.[2] The fads of coteries
and salons never had any appeal for him.

If his qualities appear in these reviews, so too do his
limitations. Smollett's *Roderick Random* incurred his
censure because it gave " no opportunity to the mind for
useful reflections, nor to the heart for good resolutions."[3]

---

[1] PO. 9, 177 and 220.   [2] PO. 9, 416.

[3] " dem Geiste aber weder zu nützlichen Betrachtungen noch dem Herze
zu guten Entschliessungen Gelegenheit geben." 6th May, 1755. (PO. 9, 401.)

This moral standpoint was a characteristic fault of the age, and one which never deserted Lessing, though his later conception of it was more profound.

After 1755 Lessing was too preoccupied with other work to produce criticisms with regularity, and only one or two isolated essays appeared in Voss' paper after that date. These reviews of Lessing's early years are in themselves unimportant ; they are of interest because they already reflect the qualities of the man. Above all they helped to develop his powers as a journalistic critic.

Not long after his appointment as reviewer, Lessing extended his field of activity still further. He began to write for Voss' newspaper a monthly supplement, dealing with current literary topics. This double sheet, entitled *The Latest from the Realm of Wit (Das Neueste aus dem Reiche des Witzes)*, appeared from April to December 1751, when it ceased publication on Lessing's departure for Wittenberg.

The Latest from the Realm of Wit contains much that shows Lessing at his worst. For once he was preoccupied with pleasing the general public, a task for which he possessed neither aptitude nor real inclination. The clumsily moral stories, published in July and August, and the dull allegory which appeared in December, are certainly among the poorest productions of Lessing's pen.

Certain numbers do nevertheless throw some light on Lessing's mind and on his attitude to literature at this date. His early criticism, like that of his fore-runners, is based on the rules of art. These rules had gradually accumulated in France in the seventeenth century and had been reduced to a system by Boileau-Despréaux in his *Art poétique* (1674). Their chief exponent in Germany in the first half of the eighteenth century was Gottsched. Though Gottsched's authority was soon attacked, the rules continued to command universal respect, for they were believed to be based on the practice of the ancients. Greek literature was rarely studied at first hand at this time and so Boileau's rules were regarded as genuinely Greek. It is not surprising that Lessing, too, proclaims his allegiance to the rules in the June number of *The Latest from the Realm of Wit*. But he adds a vital proviso—" The rules in the fine arts have arisen from observations made on their works. These observations have been multiplied from time to time and *are still being multiplied, as often as a genius, who never exactly follows his predecessors, strikes out on a new path, or continues one already known beyond its old limits.*"[1] (My italics.) The importance of this qualification cannot be overrated, for it admits a possibility of evolution in literature, which Gottsched had denied, and emancipates it from slavish imitation. It is the key to the significance of Lessing's rôle in the development of German literature.

An example of this attitude is to be found in Lessing's appreciation of the new poet, Klopstock. In the April number Lessing had mocked at Gottsched for his blind opposition to this rising genius. In May and again in September he returned to Klopstock's poetry and discussed his innovations in a long and sympathetic review. Lessing's elastic conception of the rules of art found expression throughout his life in the alacrity with which he welcomed and appreciated new works of merit.

Yet another fact of importance emerges from these essays. We have seen that Lessing was ready to pay homage to originality, but he was not to be dazzled by brilliant but unsound theory. So, in the April number, he discussed and rejected Rousseau's paradoxical opinion, that the development of the arts and sciences had been responsible for the decline of morals. " The arts," said Lessing, " are what we make them. It is our own fault if they are detrimental to us."[2] To connect the facts of

---

[1] " Die Regeln in den schönen Künsten sind aus Beobachtungen entstanden, welche man über die Werke derselben gemacht hat. Diese Beobachtungen haben sich von Zeit zu Zeit vermehret und vermehren sich noch, so oft ein Genie, welches niemals seinen Vorgängern ganz folgt einen neuen Weg einschlägt oder den schon bekannten über die alten Grenzen hinaus bähnet." (PO. 8, 47.)

[2] " Die Künste sind das, zu was wir sie machen. Es liegt nur an uns, wenn sie uns schädlich sind." (PO. 8, 30.)

the progress of knowledge and the deterioration of morals as cause and effect was, in Lessing's view, an instance of confused thinking. Against this impure reasoning (impure because it was biased by emotion) his clear scientific brain was proof.

At the early age of twenty-four, Lessing began in 1753 to publish a collected edition of his works. A good deal of manuscript work was now first presented to the public. Some of these new essays were issued in a collection of *Letters* (usually referred to as the *Kritischen Briefe* of 1753), which constituted the second volume of the works. The fictitious letter was a fashionable device to render learning more palatable and interesting. Certain letters were reprinted from *The Latest from the Realm of Wit*, but these represent only a small proportion of the volume.

Very little of the new material referred to contemporary literature. The first eight letters are important, however, in presenting a new aspect of Lessing's mind. He now appeared for the first time as a defender of unpopular causes and a guardian of unjustly tarnished reputations. These letters are devoted to a rehabilitation of Simon Lemm, a sixteenth-century poet and scholar, whose reputation had been obscured by the attacks of Martin Luther and his adherents. Lessing's defence of Lemm was successful, thanks to sound scholarship and research (these qualities are prominent in other letters of this series, notably in the criticism of Jöcher's *Gelehrten-Lexikon* in the twenty-fifth letter). The successful championship of lost causes was to be henceforth as conspicuous a feature of Lessing's writings as was his merciless destruction of exaggerated contemporary reputations.

An instance of this severity against literary incompetence occurs in these letters. In consequence of the backward state of German literature, translation of foreign books was all the rage in the first half of the eighteenth century. Both ancient and modern works were being translated into German in enormous numbers. Among these renderings was a translation of the *Odes* and *Ars poetica* of Horace issued in 1752 by S. G. Lange.[1] Lessing, a devoted admirer of the Latin poet, was shocked and outraged at the incompetence of this version. He gave vent to his indignation in a letter to Professor G. S. Nicolai :

I have noted more than two hundred such childish errors and I have prepared and am very much inclined to print a criticism of the work.[2]

The promised review appeared as the twenty-fourth of the *Letters* of 1753, and was published simultaneously in the *Hamburgische Correspondent* of 10th and 13th November, 1753. Lessing devoted the greater part of his criticism to castigating Lange for his error in translating *ducentia* as *ducenta* in the line

" Pocula Lethaeos ut si ducentia somnos,"

but he also appended a list of thirteen other grave mistakes which a schoolboy might have committed. Lange's claim that he had given a literal rendering made Lessing's task easy and gave added point to his sarcasm. The essay concluded with a complete condemnation of Lange's translation :

Let others decide whether it is strong, poetic, pure or has any other virtue. I at any rate should not know where to look to find such a quality.[3]

We are now on the threshold of the first of several controversies in which Lessing was involved. However just Lessing's criticisms were, it was not unnatural that Lange should have been angered by this attack. He accordingly prepared a reply in the form of a letter to the editors of the *Hamburgische Correspondent*. He explained

[1] Lange, born in 1711, was a pastor who already enjoyed some repute as a poet for his imitations of Horace (*Horazische Oden*, 1747). He died in 1781.

[2] " Solcher kindischen Vergehungen habe ich mehr als zweyhundert angemerkt, und ich habe Lust eine Beurtheilung seiner ganzen Arbeit, die ich schon fertig habe, drucken zu lassen." 9th June, 1752.

[3] " Ob sie stark, ob sie poetisch, ob sie rein sei, ob sie sonst eine andere Vollkommenheit besitze, das mögen andre entscheiden. Ich wenigstens wüsste nicht, wo ich sie finden sollte." (PO. 8, 177, MK. 3, 244.)

some of his errors as misprints, others he sought to defend by intricate evasions. Up to this point the dispute had been impersonal, and had not surpassed the degree of acrimony usual at that time in literary controversy. But Lange now made a false step, which was to have fatal consequences for his reputation ; he accused his adversary of a kind of literary blackmail, suggesting that Lessing had offered his criticism and his improved renderings for money, and had only published when Lange had rejected them.

This was not only unjust ; it was a grave error of judgment. Lessing was deeply hurt and dismayed by this assault upon his personal character.[1] He was always a formidable adversary when roused, and he now felt that his hard-won reputation was menaced by a base slander. He had already treated Lange with severity ; now, in sheer self-preservation, he was to become merciless. His preliminary step was to announce the appearance of Lange's letter in a review in the *Berlinische priviligierte Zeitung* of 27th December, 1753. He indicated its unexpectedly personal nature and denied the accusation in measured terms :

There is one point, about which I cannot express myself too soon. I have had to experience from him something which I should not have expected from any reasonable man, let alone from a cleric. . . . He attacks my moral character, which, I should have thought, is not called into question in grammatical disputes. . . . He makes of me a critical adventurer, who provokes a writer in order that the latter may buy his criticism off. To this I have only one answer : that I publicly declare Herr Pastor Lange to be the most malicious slanderer, unless he proves the accusation made on the above-mentioned page.[2]

---

[1] See letter to Michaelis, 10th February, 1754.

[2] " Ein einziger Punkt ist es, über welchen ich mich nicht zeitig genug erklären kann. Was ich mir nie von einem vernünftigen Manne, geschweige von einem Geistlichen vermutet hätte, muss ich von ihm erfahren, . . . Er greift meinen moralischen Charakter an, auf welchen es bei grammatikalischen Streitigkeiten, sollte ich meinen, nicht ankäme . . . er macht mich zu einem kritischen Bretteur, welcher die Schriftsteller herausfordert, damit sie ihm die Ausfoderung abkaufen sollen. Ich weiss hierauf nichts zu antworten als dieses : dass ich hier vor aller Welt den Herrn Prediger Lange für den boshaftesten Verleumder erkläre, wenn er mir die auf der angeführten Seite gemachte Beschuldigung nicht beweiset." (PO. 9, 298.)

Some idea of the serious light in which Lessing regarded the affair may be derived from the fact that he abandoned the customary anonymity and appended his name to this review.

Meanwhile Lessing pushed rapidly on with the preparation of his full reply, which was published in January 1754 as *A Vademecum for Mr. S. G. Lange, Pastor in Laublingen, prepared in this Pocket Format by Gotth. Ephr. Lessing* (*Ein Vademecum für den Hrn. Sam. Gotth. Lange, Pastor in Laublingen, in diesem Taschenformate ausgefertiget von Gotth. Ephr. Lessing*). The title derives from the small format of Lessing's works, which Lange had jeeringly termed " vademecums " or pocket-companions. The plan of this work was twofold. Lessing proposed first to substantiate and expand his criticisms of Lange's translation, and then to prove that the accusations directed against him by Lange were slanderous. The introduction showered acid contempt and bitter sarcasm on the unfortunate pastor, concluding with the insulting words

A glass of fresh spring water, to moderate the agitation of your boiling blood, will be most helpful to you before we proceed to the first sub-section. Have another, Herr Pastor ! Now let's begin.[1]

The outcome of the *Vademecum* was an easy victory for Lessing. The shortcomings of Lange's translation and the weakness of his arguments were sufficiently obvious, and Lessing's remorseless logic exposed them one by one. Now and then his ardour carried him too far, but his criticism is, in general, fair and constitutes a damning indictment ; for the list of Lange's errors grows ever longer, till the accumulation of evidence is overwhelming.

As to the personal attack, Lessing had no difficulty in rebutting it. He proved conclusively that the infamous suggestion, that he should offer his criticisms to Lange in return for a consideration, emanated from Lange's

[1] " Ein Glas frisches Brunnenwasser, die Wallung Ihres kochenden Geblüts etwas niederzuschlagen, wird Ihnen sehr dienlich sein, ehe wir zur ersten Unterabteilung schreiten. Noch eines, Herr Pastor !—Nun lassen Sie uns anfangen." (PO. 14, 50, MK. 3, 253.)

own friend, Professor G. S. Nicolai, and that he, Lessing, had ignored it.

Lessing has sometimes been censured for the virulent tone of this little book, though unfairly. One should recall the provocation under which he wrote. It was Lange who descended into the sphere of personalities ; and he reaped his reward. Lessing's essay, crushing though it is, does not requite calumny with calumny. He overwhelms Lange with deserved contempt and obloquy, but Lange's personal character is untouched, except as the author of a slanderous statement.

The result of the dispute was the destruction of Lange's renown, such as it was, and the enhancement of Lessing's reputation as a critic to be respected and feared.

Lessing's insistence on accurate translation involved him four years later in another literary quarrel. This time Lieberkühn's rendering of the *Idylls* of Theocritus, Moschus and Bion was the provocation. Lessing detected that this was not a translation of the Greek original, but of a Latin version. Such renderings at second-hand were always an abomination to Lessing, and in a letter to Moses Mendelssohn he expressed his indignation :

You cannot imagine what stupid stuff Lieberkühn has written ! He has translated from the Latin version and has not even understood that ! [1]

In due course a scathing review of the work appeared in F. Nicolai's periodical, *Bibliothek der schönen Wissenschaften und der freien Künste*. Lessing's tone is less virulent here than in the *Vademecum*, for this dispute remained entirely on a literary plane. It is nevertheless a vehement piece of writing. The clue to its vigour is to be found in a letter of Lessing to F. Nicolai :

With regard to the ancient writers, I am a true knight errant ; my

---

[1] " Sie können sich nicht einbilden, was Lieberkühn für dummes Zeug gemacht hat ! Er hat aus der lateinischen Übersetzung übersetzt und auch nicht einmal diese verstanden." December 1757.

blood boils at once, when I see them so wretchedly maltreated.[1]

Enthusiasm for the ancients was, however, only partly responsible for Lessing's strong feelings about these two translations. His deep seriousness of purpose underlies both controversies. He did not merely despise incompetence in literature ; he thought it dangerous. Hence his ruthless treatment of careless, superficial or ignorant work, whether original or translation. This quality makes him the most powerful critical force in the rise of German literature in the eighteenth century.

3. THE LITERATURBRIEFE

Lessing's years of journalism in Berlin had so far been years of preparation. He had forged himself a sword, which he was now to wield in the most important critical campaign of his life. Campaign is indeed the only possible term for the so-called *Literaturbriefe* or *Letters concerning the most recent Literature (Briefe, die neueste Litteratur betreffend)*. In these letters, which began to appear in 1759, Lessing appears at his full stature, a solitary giant, challenging and conquering, judging and executing, unaided and unsupported. Nicolai and Mendelssohn collaborated, but throughout 1759 Lessing was responsible for two-thirds of the letters.

The fictitious letter had been employed by Lessing already in the *Critical Letters* of 1753. This new series purported to be addressed to a wounded officer (the Seven Years' War had then been in progress for three years), who desired to be kept in touch with contemporary literature. In this fiction Lessing may well have had in mind his soldier friend, Ewald von Kleist.

Lessing's *Literaturbriefe* present a cross-section of the German literature of his age. The opening letters deal once more with bad translations. German versions of

---

[1] " In Ansehung der alten Schriftsteller, bin ich ein wahrer irrender Ritter ; die Galle läuft mir gleich über, wenn ich sehe, dass man sie so jämmerlich misshandelt." 21st January, 1758.

Pope, Gay and Bolingbroke meet with more or less drastic condemnation. Wieland then receives Lessing's attention (Letters 7–13). Lessing justly doubts the sincerity of the *Empfindungen eines Christen* and attacks what he ironically terms Wieland's " patriotic contempt for his own nation."[1] Nine months later (Letters 63 and 64) he exposes Wieland's plagiary of Shore in the play *Lady Johanna Gray*. The famous seventeenth Letter and the eighty-first treat of the state of the German theatre.[2] He warmly defends Klopstock's poetry (Letters 19 and 51), but points out that excessive sensibility is its chief defect (Letter 111). In the thirty-second Letter he cordially welcomes a new poet, Gerstenberg. The fashionable combination of theology with rationalism is vigorously denounced in Letters 49 and romantic history condemned in Letter 52.

In two letters he makes important observations on the nature of poetry. The nineteenth Letter contains the statement—" Rules are what the masters of art choose to observe."[3] His attitude to the rules is still unchanged;[4] they are not *à priori* laws, but are derived from the work of the genius. In the fifty-first Letter he acknowledges that lyric poetry is a matter rather of feeling than of logical thinking ; this was an important pronouncement for an age which expected a moral from all forms of literature.

Lessing also foreshadows in the thirty-third Letter the work which Herder was later to do for the folk-song. He writes an appreciation of a Lapp song, which had been translated, and claims, a decade before Herder," that poets are born in every zone and that vivid sentiments are no prerogative of civilized peoples."[5]

---

[1] " Patriotische Verachtung seiner Nation." (PO. 4, 43.)

[2] See below, p. 59.

[3] " Was die Meister der Kunst zu beobachten für gut befinden, das sind Regeln." (PO. 4, 65.)

[4] See above, p. 44.

[5] " Dass unter jedem Himmelsstriche Dichter geboren werden und dass lebhafte Empfindungen kein Vorrecht gesitteter Völker sind." (PO. 4, 87.)

This cursory survey of the contents of the *Literatur-briefe* indicates the variety of their scope. It can, however, give no idea of their importance. Gottsched and the Swiss had set themselves up as critical dictators, but as they lacked the necessary gifts, they did at least as much harm as good. Lessing now came forward to take the place which they could not fill. His judgment was sound; his flexible mind was ready to appreciate genius in whatever form it might appear; his views on the rules of art were not rigid, but evolutionary. Thirty years old, and at the height of his powers, Lessing was able to further a sound taste in a public which needed guidance in the rapidly developing literature of Germany. In his hands, for just on two years the *Literaturbriefe* denounced mediocrity, applauded genius and cultivated an accurate and sensitive taste in the German public.

CHAPTER V

LESSING'S CRITICISM AND THE DRAMA

1. BEGINNINGS

LESSING's services to German literature were greatest in the sphere of the drama. His first interest in Leipzig had been the theatre ; and so, when he decided to live by his pen in Berlin, it was the theatre which was the first subject of his journalism. In collaboration with his friend, Mylius, he began in 1750 to issue a quarterly periodical with the title, *Contributions to the History and Encouragement of the Theatre (Beyträge zur Historie und Aufnahme des Theaters)*. The programme of this magazine, as announced in the preface, was nothing if not ambitious. Its chief aims were : to inculcate the principles of taste by an examination of works of criticism and to provide models for the German theatre by means of translations of plays from Greek, Latin, French, Italian, English, Spanish and Dutch.

It is not surprising that this extravagant promise on the part of an inexperienced young man of twenty-one remained unfulfilled. The preface contains, however, more than this. At a moment when the English dramatists were scarcely known in Germany and the tyranny of French taste still prevailed, Lessing did not hesitate to affirm that the German's natural bent would, if he chose to follow it, bring him nearer to the English theatre than to the French.[1] "Shakespeare, Dryden, Wycherley, Vanbrugh, Cibber, Congreve are poets barely known to us by more than name, and yet they deserve our respect just as much as the esteemed French poets."[2] The

[1] " Das ist gewiss, wollte der Deutsche in der dramatischen Poesie seinem eignen Naturelle folgen, so würde unsere Schaubühne mehr der englischen als französischen gleichen." (PO. 7, 29).

[2] " Shakespeare, Dryden, Wicherley, Vanbrugh, Cibber, Congreve sind Dichter, die man fast bei uns nur dem Namen nach kennet, und gleichwohl verdienen sie unsere Hochachtung sowohl als die gepriesenen französischen Dichter." (PO. 7, 28.)

baldness of this list of names of English dramatists of
such unequal merit suggests that Lessing's own acquaintance with them was as yet not much more profound than
that which he attributed to the public. But he was on
the right road, and his industry soon provided him with
the necessary first-hand knowledge.

The *Contributions* were too short-lived (only four
numbers appeared) for there to be any correspondence
between the ambitious plan and the work itself. Lessing
began with a brief treatise on the life and works of
Plautus, whom he had recently both studied and imitated.[1]
This was followed by a translation of the *Captivi* of
Plautus, which, as his prefatory remarks show, he
intended to serve as a model for German comedy.

In the next number appeared an essay, in which the
germ of much of his later critical method is clearly seen.
Lessing had received a letter disagreeing with the
favourable view of Plautus which he had taken in the
first number. Lessing quotes this letter, which is based
on the standpoint of French classicism, in full. It is a
well-known fact that Lessing's most effective critical work
resulted usually from the stimulus of some contradiction;
in this essay appears the first tentative effort of the young
writer publicly to refute an opponent. His power of
rapid assimilation and analysis is clearly perceptible in his
summary of his adversary's objections. His defence of
Plautus' morals and humour is successful. With regard
to the Roman dramatist's technique he is less happy.
Lessing had only lately escaped from Leipzig, dominated
by the francophile taste of Gottsched. As the preface to
the *Contributions* shows, he was beginning to react
against the restrictions of French classicism, but he had
not as yet openly revolted. And so, though he felt that
Plautus was a good dramatist in spite of neglect of the
rules, he was not able to justify this view theoretically.
He is therefore driven to evasions in order to explain
away Plautus' infringement of the three unities. The

[1] See below, p. 114.

narrowness of his views at this time is apparent too in his remarks on the aim of comedy, which is " to form and improve the manners of the spectators."[1]

This brief controversy was of great value to Lessing. In his original essay he had made rash and inaccurate statements. When these were pointed out by his opponent, he was man enough to admit them candidly, but in future he gave very great attention to avoiding the recurrence of such defects and always prepared his critical work with the greatest care, a task in which his phenomenal capacity for reading and for turning his reading to practical account was of inestimable value to him. It is this thoroughness which accounts for the tone of certainty so characteristic of his mature work, and this early experience was of the greatest importance to him as a warning and a stimulus.

The vigour and emphasis of his style, when bad work or a contradiction gave him an impetus, is evident in his last essay in this quarterly, a review of a new translation of Samuel Werenfels' *Speech in defence of Plays*. After praising the original, he abuses the translation on the grounds that a good version exists already, that Gregorius, the translator, does not understand the Latin of the original, that he cannot write German and that his notes are bad. Gregorius came from Lessing's native town, Kamenz, but the only extant reference to him in the letters shows Lessing's anger confined to the literary field. On 2nd November, 1750, he wrote to his father, " I send you herewith the third number of the theatrical Contributions, in which you will find Mr. Gregorius duly honoured. The review is by me and I am only sorry that I have not made it still more severe. If I had chosen to make myself known with such stuff as he writes, I should have written whole folios by now."[2]

[1] " die Sitten der Zuschauer zu bilden und zu bessern." (PO. 13, 159.)

[2] " Ich sende Ihnen hierbey das dritte Stück der theatralischen Beyträge, worinne Sie des H. Gregorius in Ehren gedacht finden. Die Recension ist von mir, und es dauert mich nur, dass ich sie nicht noch ärger gemacht habe Hätte ich mich durch solch Zeug bekant machen wollen, als er thut, so wollte ich schon ganze Folianten geschrieben haben."

Lessing soon abandoned the *Contributions*, the standard of which had been lowered by the unsound essays of his flippant and unconscientious collaborator Mylius.[1] Unimportant though the work may be, he had gained extremely valuable experience.

2. MATURING VIEWS. 1754-8

Lessing's journalistic activities continued uninterrupted from 1750 onwards, but it was not until 1754 that he again concerned himself expressly with the theatre. In that year he began to publish a periodical under the title *Theatrical Library* (*Theatralische Bibliothek*), which was avowedly a continuation of the earlier *Contributions*. The plan outlined in the preface was, however, much more restrained than had been that of the earlier publication. The number of volumes was to be limited and the work to constitute " not merely a theatrical hotchpotch, but really a critical history of the theatre."[2]

Lessing's work in this periodical shows a very interesting advance. He has not yet entirely rejected French classical tragedy, as his account (in the third essay) of a Spanish tragedy on the French model proves, but his attitude is considerably more sceptical than it had been three years before, as is evident in his sarcastic review of Crébillon's *Thyeste* and the accompanying criticism of the French tendency to insert a high-flown love-intrigue into any and every classical theme.[3]

The positive side of his criticism appears at once in the first essay. Changes in the drama were taking place, consisting of the sentimentalization of comedy (*comédie larmoyante*) and the introduction of middle-class characters as heroes of tragedy (domestic tragedy or *bürgerliches Trauerspiel*). The former was a French product,

---

[1] See Lessing's preface to the *Theatralische Bibliothek*. (PO. 7, 43.)

[2] " nicht bloss einen theatralischen Mischmasch, sondern wirklich eine kritische Geschichte des Theaters . . ." (PO. 7, 44.)

[3] *Von den Trauerspielen des Seneca*. (PO. 13, 223.)

the latter English.   In his first essay, Lessing proposed to consider the new " tearful " comedy, adopting the interesting method of quoting in full an essay for and one against (by the German Gellert and the Frenchman Chassiron respectively), finally playing the arbiter himself.   His verdict is in favour of the *comédie larmoyante* as it was practised by Gellert, on the ground that the combination of the comic and the touching is more realistic than the presentation of one of these only.

The most important aspect of this periodical lies in the increased attention devoted to the English theatre. Already in the essay on the *comédie larmoyante* Lessing had mentioned the new domestic tragedy of the English.[1] The second essay now contained an account (at second-hand) of the life of an English tragic dramatist, James Thomson, better known as the author of *The Seasons*. Lessing's interest was further maintained by a brief and sympathetic history of the English stage, written by his friend F. Nicolai, and published as the twelfth essay.

The periodical exhibits, too, Lessing's limitations at this time.   He objects to the *Hercules furiosus* of Seneca, because the very virtues and heroic actions of Hercules incense the gods.   The moralizing view of art and literature, which Lessing shared with his rationalistic age, had no place in its scheme of tragedy for the apparently undeserved anger of the gods.   This was the era of belief in a wise and providential ordering of the universe, and in a rigid chain of cause and effect.   For the eighteenth century the gods must be just and their anger must have a perceptible cause.   Virtue must, if possible, be rewarded and must at any rate not entail the destruction of the virtuous character.   Lessing's view of tragedy, expressed in the essay on Seneca, is a compromise between the standpoint of his own age and the just instinct which made him respect tragedies transcending the limitations of the eighteenth century :

Actually I do not consider it a necessity that a good lesson should

[1] PO. 12, 161.

E

emerge from the plot of a tragedy, provided that various passages teach us useful truths. However it is at any rate necessary that one should not be able to deduce an evil lesson from it.[1]

This passage denotes an important step forward, for the tragedy, *as a whole*, is now freed from the necessity of moralizing.

Lessing never loses sight of the practical aspect of criticism ; this series of essays has the purpose, like its predecessor the *Contributions*, of modelling the taste of the public and of furthering the writing of good plays. This is particularly evident in the summaries of unprinted Italian plays,[2] which were intended to be " as it were an arsenal for our comic poets."[3]

The essays of the *Theatrical Library* had mirrored Lessing's critical development and had implied, in the increasing attention devoted to the English, his gradual emancipation from the rules of French classicism. His first definite break with these rules occurs in a minor work, the preface to the German version of Thomson's tragedies. Here he declared that " knowledge of the human heart . . . the magic art of causing every passion to arise, grow and break out before our eyes . . . no Aristotle or Corneille can teach, though Corneille did not lack it."[4] " All their other rules " he goes on to say, " can at most produce nothing but pedantic twaddle."[5] And now Lessing mentions Addison's *Cato* and Lillo's play together and unhesitatingly gives his approval to the less " correct " but more moving *London Merchant*.

---

[1] " Eigentlich halte ich es eben für keine Notwendigkeit, dass aus der Fabel eines Trauerspiels eine gute Lehre fliessen müsse, wenn uns nur einzelne Stellen von nützlichen Wahrheiten unterrichten. Allein so viel wird doch wenigstens notwendig sein, dass man auch keine böse Lehre daraus folgern könne." (PO. 13, 189.)

[2] *Essay XIV.*

[3] " gleichsam ein Magazin für unsere komische Dichter." (PO. 12, 386.)

[4] " Kenntnis des menschlichen Herzens . . . die magische Kunst, jede Leidenschaft vor unsern Augen entstehen, wachsen und ausbrechen zu lassen . . . , die kein Aristoteles, kein Corneille lehrt, ob sie gleich dem Corneille selbst nicht fehlte." (PO. 7, 87.)

[5] " Alle ihre übrigen Regeln können aufs höchste nichts als ein schulmässiges Gewäsche hervorbringen." (*Ibid.*)

Lastly the purpose of tragedy is now no longer to instruct but to move—" These tears of pity and of sympathetic humanity alone are the aim of tragedy or it can have none at all."[1]   Genuine artistic creation and the emotions have supplanted the rules of the French and the exclusive right of the logical intellect.

3. The Decisive Step

Lessing's gradual rejection of French principles in the theatre and his increasing admiration for the English drama finally came to a head, after a long evolution, in the famous seventeenth *Literaturebrief*.   This is at once a final settlement with Gottsched and a positive declaration for the guidance of German drama, and it provides in a small framework a perfect example of the way in which Lessing is never content with purely negative, destructive criticism but invariably passes on to some practical proposition.

The opening is a magnificent example of the directness of his attack without prelude, preamble or superfluity of any kind.   As usual a statement with which he disagrees serves as a spring-board.   " ' Nobody,' say the authors of the *Bibliothek*, ' will deny that the German stage owes a great deal of its early improvement to Professor Gottsched.'   I am this nobody.   I deny it categorically.   It would have been better if Herr Gottsched had never meddled with the theatre.   His supposed improvements either concern trifles or are really retrograde steps."[2]   Reasons for this assertion follow, based on Gottsched's method.   Firstly it was purely imitative—" He understood a little French and began to translate ; he encouraged any and everyone who could rhyme and

[1] " Nur diese Tränen des Mitleids und der sich fühlenden Menschlichkeit sind die Absicht des Trauerspiels, oder es kann gar keine haben." (PO. 7, 88.)

[2] " ' Niemand,' sagen die Verfasser der Bibliothek, ' wird leugnen, dass die deutsche Schaubühne einen grossen Teil ihrer ersten Verbesserung dem Herrn Professor Gottsched zu danken habe.'   Ich bin dieser Niemand ; ich leugne es geradezu.   Es wäre zu wünschen, dass sich Herr Gottsched niemals mit dem Theater vermengt hätte." (P.O. 9. 47).

understand ' Oui, Monsieur' to translate too "[1]
secondly he chose for his imitation totally unsuitable
models—" he wanted not merely to be the improver of
our old drama, but to be the creator of an entirely new
one. And what kind of new one? Of one on French
lines ; he did not stop to investigate whether this drama
on French lines was appropriate to German habits of
thought or not."[2] With that the purely destructive
attack is concluded and in a brief transition Lessing
passes on to the steps which Gottsched might and ought
to have taken. " He could have observed easily enough
from our old plays, which he banished, that we rather fall
in with the taste of the English than of the French."[3]
The German prefers the terrible to the tender and wishes
to see more action on the stage than is permitted in
French tragedy.

Among all the English dramatists it is Shakespeare
who would have been the best model, and his introduction to the German stage would have had far more
favourable consequences than the attempted popularization of Corneille and Racine.

Lessing now takes his leave of Gottsched and proceeds
to elaborate his praise of Shakespeare. " Even if one
decides the matter in accordance with the models of the
ancients, Shakespeare is a far greater tragic dramatist than
Corneille, although the latter was well acquainted with
ancients and the former scarcely at all. Corneille
approaches them in technique, Shakespeare in essence. . . .
After the *Oedipus* of Sophocles no play in the world can
have more power over our passions than *Othello, King*

---

[1] " Er verstand ein wenig Französisch und fing an zu übersetzen ; er ermun-
terte alles, was reimen und ' Oui, Monsieur' verstehen konnte, gleichfalls zu
übersetzen." (PO. 4, 55).

[2] " er wollte nicht sowohl unser altes Theater verbessern, als der Schöpfer
eines ganz neuen sein. Und was für eines neuen ? Eines französierenden ;
ohne zu untersuchen, ob dieses französierende Theater der deutschen Denkung-
sart angemessen sei oder nicht." (PO. 4, 57.)

[3] " Er hätte aus unserm alten dramatischen Stücken, welche er vertrieb, hinlänglich abmerken können, dass wir mehr in den Geschmack der Engländer
als der Franzosen einschlagen." (PO. 4, 57.)

Lear, Hamlet, etc."[1]   Destructive criticism has now
yielded to positive suggestion.   Lessing now shows a
more extensive and profound knowledge of Shakespeare, but at the same time reveals limitations.   The
rules of the French no longer have validity, but an external criterion for the judgment of Shakespeare (or of any
other writer) is still a necessity for him.   This criterion is
now the work of the Greeks, from whom the rules of the
French had been drawn, however distorted their interpretation may have been.   Lessing has gone to the
original source, but the fixed criterion remains.   A second
interesting point reveals the traditionless state of German
drama at the time.   Although Lessing rejects Gottsched's pedestrian imitation, he himself recommends
another more suitable model for emulation.

All this is constructive enough, but Lessing goes
further and appends to the essay a scene in prose from
what he claims to be an old German play on the theme of
Faust.   Actually it is his own work and he thus goes to
the extreme limit of the practical by giving an example of
German drama as it might be.   The very pretence that it
is drawn from an old German play is an attempt to
encourage German dramatists to investigate their past
dramatic literature, to rehabilitate its reputation and to
remedy the lack of a tradition.

After this brilliant essay Lessing concerned himself but
little with the drama in the *Literaturbriefe.*   Only in the
fifty-first did he return to the comparison of Shakespeare
with the French, where he praises the vigour and suit-
ability of his style to the characters in preference to the
correctness of Racine—" Hence it is indeed a great
achievement in a tragic poet, if he clothes the most sublime thoughts in the most common words and causes his

---

[1] " Auch nach den Mustern der Alten die Sache zu entscheiden, ist Shakes-
peare ein weit grösserer tragischer Dichter als Corneille, obgleich dieser die
Alten sehr wohl und jener fast gar nicht gekannt hat.   Corneille kömmt ihnen
in der mechanischen Einrichtung und Shakespeare in dem Wesentlichen näher
. . . Nach dem Oedipus des Sophokles muss in der Welt kein Stück mehr
Gewalt über unsere Leidenschaften haben als Othello, als König Lear, als
Hamlet etc."   (PO. 4, 57-8.)

characters under the stress of emotion to seize upon not the most noble but the most emphatic word, even if it should have a somewhat vulgar subsidiary meaning. They will indeed know little of this achievement however, who only find the correct Racine to their taste and are unfortunate enough not to be acquainted with Shakespeare."[1]

It is the seventeenth *Literaturbrief*, analysed above, which is Lessing's most decisive step in his criticism of the drama and the theatre. Although the preface to Thomson's tragedies had reasserted the rights of powerful emotions in tragedy that essay could reach only a small public in comparison with a journalistic enterprise like the *Literaturbriefe*. Moreover the seventeenth *Literaturebrief* champions Shakespeare instead of the English sentimental tragedy of the eighteenth century; and it is written in the incisive style and with the tone of certainty based on knowledge, which is the characteristic of Lessing at this highest point of his career as a journalistic critic.

4. THE FINAL SYSTEM

During the greater part of the next seven years Lessing was in Breslau earning good money as the Secretary of General Tauentzien but doing comparatively little literary work. His only contact with the theatre was the writing of his comedy, *Minna von Barnhelm*. In 1767, however, he was back in Berlin obliged once more to live by his pen. It will be recalled that at this time an attempt was being made to found a national theatre in Hamburg and Lessing was invited to join this enterprise as official theatre dramatist and critic. As vehicle for his

---

[1] " Es ist daher sogar ein grosses Kunststück eines tragischen Dichters, wenn er besonders die erhabensten Gedanken in die gemeinsten Worte kleidet und im Affekte nicht das edelste, sondern das nachdrücklichste Wort, wenn es auch schon einen etwas niedrigen Nebenbegriff mit sich führen sollte, ergreifen lässt. Von diesem Kunststücke werden aber freilich diejenigen nichts wissen wollen die nur an einem korrekten Racine Geschmack finden und so unglücklich sind, keinen Shakespeare zu kennen." (PO. 4, 152.)

reviews he issued a periodical, the *Hamburg Dramaturgy* (*Hamburgische Dramaturgie*).

Lessing began his new work without any very great expectations[1] and without any very great interest.   The tone of the preface which appeared under the date 22nd April, 1767, the day on which the theatre was opened, betrays no such vigour and enthusiasm as had marked the inauguration of the *Literaturbriefe*.   After deploring in a few words the poor state of the German theatre, Lessing announced that his periodical would contain a critical register of all the plays produced in the Hamburg theatre, and would devote itself to the criticism of actors as well as of dramatists.   His scepticism over the new theatre was soon justified.   Intrigues and discord were rife.[2]   Lessing's dissatisfaction is revealed in his correspondence.   " You can imagine," he wrote to Nicolai in August, " that I scribble this rag unwillingly ; and I hope it will be evident to you from it.   I know that it is worthless."[3]

In spite of the unfavourable view held by Lessing himself, there are many excellent observations in the early numbers of the *Dramaturgy* ; as, for example, the rejection of the Christian hero in tragedy, on the ground that his confident hope of a happy after-life deprives his fate of tragic effect.[4]   Lessing's interest in the work gradually became keener.   Opposition among the actors had caused him, as he states in the twenty-fifth number, to abandon the intention of including the acting in his criticism.   This, together with the fact that he was soon very much behindhand in his articles on the plays performed, led him before long to give up any attempt to keep pace with the productions of the theatre.   Consequently he was now able to expand at leisure on any

[1] See letter to Gleim, 1st February, 1767.

[2] See letter to his brother Karl, 22nd June, 1767.

[3] " Dass ich ungern diesen Wisch schmiere, können Sie glauben ; und Sie werden es ihm hoffentlich ansehen.   Ich weiss es, dass nichts daran ist."   4th August, 1767.

[4] 2, Stück.

particular play which gave him an opportunity for general
reflections on the drama.

From the tenth number on, another and more
important factor sharpened Lessing's interest in the
Dramaturgy. To produce his best critical work he always
needed something with which he disagreed profoundly
and which stimulated him to contradiction. This he
now found in the French drama and in particular Voltaire.
In number seventy, he candidly states that this polemical
method has been the foundation of the *Dramaturgy*—
" Let a critical writer . . . first seek out someone with
whom he can quarrel. Thus he will gradually get into
his subject and the rest will follow as a matter of course.
I frankly admit that I have selected primarily the French
writers for this purpose, and among them particularly
M. de Voltaire."[1]   And certainly the tone of the *Dramaturgy* is far more vivid, the ideas expressed profounder
and more original after Lessing has begun to tilt at
Voltaire.

Lessing's criticism of the French drama cannot be
isolated from the rest of the work for it forms part of his
familiar process of proceeding from destructive to
practical criticism. Two points in this connection,
however, may be mentioned here. Apart from reasons
embodied in the nature and spirit of French drama he has
three very powerful objections to that nation. Firstly
because of its arrogance. It should be remembered that
during the seventeenth century the French had been
easily the strongest nation in Europe and had enjoyed a
most flourishing artistic culture. The result had been a
conceit, a self-satisfaction and a contempt for their
neighbours which are reflected in the celebrated question
propounded by Father Bouhours as to whether it were
possible for a German to be a bel-esprit. With such

---

[1] " Ein kritischer Schriftsteller . . . suche sich nur erst jemanden, mit dem er
streiten kann : so kömmt er nach und nach in die Materie und das übrige findet
sich.   Hierzu habe ich mir in diesem Werke, ich bekenne es aufrichtig, nun
einmal die französischen Skribenten vornehmlich erwählet, und unter diesen
besonders den Herrn von Voltaire." (PO. 5, 297. MK. 5, 231.)

arrogance Lessing has no patience. Voltaire's assertion in the preface to *Sémiramis* that the Greeks could have learned much in tragedy from the French, is made to look as ridiculous as it deserves.[1] But he expresses himself even more fully on French conceit in artistic matters, in No. 81. "Scarcely had Corneille extricated their theatre somewhat from its primitive barbarity, than they began to believe it already near perfection ; Racine seemed to them to have added the final touch . . . for a hundred years they have deceived themselves and in part their neighbours as well."[2]

His second objection is against their slipshod and even dishonest treatment of sources and authorities, a subject on which he had already expressed himself in the *Treatises on the Fable*. In this same No. 81 Lessing reproaches Corneille with his distortion of the rules given by Aristotle in the *Poetics*. "What however does Corneille do with them? He propounds them falsely and one-sidedly enough and because he still finds them too strict, he seeks in one after the other ' some modification, some favourable interpretation ' ; he emasculates and mutilates, interprets and frustrates each —and why ? ' so as not to be forced to condemn many poems which we have seen succeed in our theatres.' A fine reason ! "[3]

Thirdly, Lessing detests the prestige the French enjoyed in Germany and its ill effect on German play-wrights. Even at the conclusion of the *Dramaturgy* he still sees this influence as strong as ever—" We are still the sworn imitators of everything foreign, particularly of

[1] 10, Stück.

[2] " Kaum riss Corneille ihr Theater ein wenig aus der Barbarei so glaubten sie es der Vollkommenheit schon ganz nahe. Racine schien ihnen die letzte Hand angelegt zu haben . . . Hundert Jahre haben Sie sich selbst, und zum Teil ihre Nachbarn mit hintergangen." (PO. 5, 336. MK. 5, 280.)

[3] " Was aber macht Corneille damit ? Er trägt sie falsch und schielend genug vor ; und weil er sie doch noch viel zu strenge findet, so sucht er bei einer nach der andern ' quelque modération, quelque favorable interprétation ' ; entkräftet und verstümmelt, deutelt und vereitelt eine jede—und warum ? ' pour ne pas être obligés de condamner beaucoup de poèmes que nous avons vus réussir sur nos théâtres ' . . . Eine schöne Ursache ! " (PO. 5, 337).

the French, whom we can never admire enough ; everything which comes to us from beyond the Rhine is
beautiful, charming, lovely, divine ; we would rather
deny the evidence of eyes and ears than find it otherwise."[1]   This third reason is really the fundamental one ;
it was the unfavourable influence exerted by the French
on his own countrymen in literature which really
prompted his onslaughts against them.   In spite of the
pessimism which he betrays in the concluding numbers of
the *Dramaturgy*, the French influence had ceased to count
among the leading spirits and was on the wane with the
great mass of the reading and theatre-going public.
This development was largely Lessing's own work.

As in the seventeenth *Literaturbrief*, Shakespeare is
advanced in sharp contrast to the French.   After dis-
missing Voltaire's use of a ghost in *Sémiramis*, Lessing
affirms that the poet must have the power of making us
believe in his creations, whatever our convictions outside
the theatre may be.   " Such a poet is Shakespeare, and
scarcely any other.   Before the ghost in *Hamlet* our hair
stands on end, whether it covers a credulous or incredu-
lous brain."[2]   The most striking praise of Shakespeare
occurs in No. 73.   Here at last he acknowledges
Shakespeare as unique and no longer subjects him
to comparison with the ancients.   " On the least of his
beauties a seal is set which exclaims to the whole world :
I am Shakespeare's ! "[3]   The limitations of Lessing's
own age, its moral preoccupation in art and its prosaic
attitude were obstacles which prevented him from

[1] " Wir sind noch immer die geschwornen Nachahmer alles Ausländischen,
besonders noch immer die untertänigen Bewunderer der nie genug bewunderten
Franzosen ; alles, was uns von jenseit dem Rheine kömmt, ist schön, reizend,
allerliebst, göttlich ; lieber verleugnen wir Gesicht und Gehör, als dass wir es
anders finden sollten." (PO. 5, 410.)

[2] " So ein Dichter ist Shakespeare, und Shakespeare fast einzig und allein.
Vor seinem Gespenste im ' Hamlet ' richten sich die Haare zu Berge, sie mögen
ein gläubiges oder ungläubiges Gehirn bedecken." (PO. 5, 67.   MK. 4, 387.)

[3] "Auf die geringste von seinen Schönheiten ist ein Stempel gedruckt, welcher
gleich der ganzen Welt zuruft : ich bin Shakespeare ! " (PO. 5, 307.   MK. 5,
243.)

making any practical use of his study of Shakespeare in his dramatic work, but in his recognition of Shakespeare's qualities Lessing had done much to prepare the way for the phase of uncritical adulation which characterized the *Sturm und Drang*, which was actually developing as the *Dramaturgie* drew to a close. It may also justifiably be maintained that his praise of Shakespeare, which was the result of close examination and gradual conviction, was healthier and sounder than the wild and unconditional eulogies of his successors.

The interest of the *Dramaturgy*, however, lies chiefly in Lessing's views on the theory of the drama. According to his own explicit statement the work was not intended to incorporate a system[1] and it is quite true that the important observations it contains occur here and there in haphazard fashion just as the consideration of various plays produced at the theatre in Hamburg gave Lessing an opportunity to raise and expound questions of theory.

One of the first points which Lessing discusses in full is the attitude of the tragic dramatist to history. The tragic dramatist, he says in No. 19, "uses a story, not because it has happened, but because it happened in such a way that he could scarcely invent it better for his present purpose."[2] Inherent probability is what matters, not the fact that the incidents have actually occurred. All this is directed against the French preference for historical subjects, a preference which dates from Corneille. Historical subjects are therefore by no means indispensable. Moreover, should the dramatist adopt an historical plot he is by no means obliged to adhere to the strict details of events, for " only the characters are sacred to him "[3]; and again

[1] 95, Stück. (PO. 5, 388. MK. 5, 348.)

[2] " braucht eine Geschichte nicht darum, weil sie geschehen ist, sondern darum, weil sie so geschehen ist, dass er sie schwerlich zu seinem gegenwärtigen Zwecke besser erdichten könnte." (PO. 5, 96. MK. 4, 426.)

[3] " nur die Charaktere sind ihm heilig," 23, Stück. (PO. 5, 113. MK. 4, 449.)

" tragedy is not history in dialogue ; history is for
tragedy only a store-house of names with which we are
accustomed to associate certain characters."[1]   And even
then it is more excusable to allot to historical persons a
character other than the traditional one than to render
them inconsistent.[2] History is therefore something
quite incidental to tragedy, the aim of which is to show
us not " what this or that individual man *has* done, but
what every man of a particular character would do in
particular given circumstances."[3] These views are in
part conditioned by Lessing's own times, with their
stress upon the man of the present and consequent
relative neglect of history ; they nevertheless embody
much sound common-sense.

In No. 34 Lessing gives a most interesting moral
interpretation of the idea of genius. His conception of the untaught genius represents an enormous
advance on the ideas current in his youth and brings him
within sight as it were of the succeeding generation,
whose leaders were Goethe and Herder—" Genius may
be allowed not to know a thousand things that every
schoolboy knows. Its strength lies not in what is
stored up by its memory, but in what it is able to produce
out of itself, out of its own emotions.'[4] Now follows
the vital definition of genius—the genius combines
" the aim of teaching what we should do and not do ; the
aim of making us acquainted with the true signs of good
and evil, of propriety and absurdity ; the aim of showing
the former as beautiful and happy even in misfortune and

---

[1] " Die Tragödie ist keine dialogierte Geschichte ; die Geschichte ist für die
Tragödie nur ein Repertorium von Namen, mit denen wir gewisse Charaktere zu
verbinden gewohnt sind." 24, Stück. (PO. 5, 115. MK. 4, 451.)

[2] 34, Stück.

[3] " was dieser oder jener einzelne Mensch getan hat, sondern was ein jeder
Mensch von einem gewissen Charakter unter gewissen gegebenen Umständen
tun werde." 19, Stück. (PO. 5, 96. MK. 4, 426.)

[4] " Dem Genie ist es vergönnt, tausend Dinge nicht zu wissen, die jeder
Schulknabe weiss ; nicht der erworbene Vorrat seines Gedächtnisses, sondern
das, was es aus sich selbst, aus seinem eignen Gefühl hervorzubringen vermag
macht seinen Reichtum aus." (PO. 5, 152. MK. 5, 46).

of showing the latter as ugly and unhappy even in good
fortune ; the aim, in themes where no immediate emulation or deterrence is involved for us, of at least occupying
our impulses of desire and abhorrence with appropriate
objects, and of placing these objects constantly in their
true light, so that no false appearance may deceive us into
desiring what we should abhor and abhorring what we
should desire."[1]   The genius according to this definition
is endowed with an instinctive moral sense as a part of
his artistic ability.

In proclaiming the instinctive rightness of the genius'
work Lessing has reached a conclusion with which
subsequent ages have agreed.   In restricting it, however,
to the moral sphere he betrays his limitation.   This
limitation lies not so much in the preoccupation with the
moral sphere, but in the exclusively *conscious* attitude to
morals.   It is our conscious moral position which he
would make the business of the genius.   Had he had at
his disposal a more subtle psychology which admitted the
value of unconscious phenomena, his view would not
differ so much from that which we hold to-day.   But this
psychological limitation is decisive and invalidates his
attitude for modern times.   Nevertheless he has made
a great step forward ; for, in his view, though the effect
of the work of art is conscious, its creation is in part
unconscious, as the remarks on the untaught instinct of
genius, quoted above, imply.

The most famous part of the *Dramaturgy* is that in
which Lessing provides a theoretical justification for the
" domestic tragedy " (*bürgerliches Trauerspiel*) by means of

---

[1] " die Absicht, uns zu unterrichten, was wir zu tun oder zu lassen haben ; die
Absicht, uns mit den eigentlichen Merkmalen des Guten und Bösen, des An-
ständigen und Lächerlichen bekannt zu machen ; die Absicht, uns jenes in allen
seinen Verbindungen und Folgen als schön und als glücklich selbst im Unglücke,
dieses hingegen als hässlich und unglücklich selbst im Glücke, zu zeigen ; die
Absicht, bei Vorwürfen, wo keine unmittelbare Nacheiferung, keine unmittelbare Abschreckung für uns statt hat, wenigstens unsere Begehrungs-und Verab-
scheuungskräfte mit solchen Gegenständen zu beschäftigen, die es zu sein
verdienen, und diese Gegenstände jederzeit in ihr wahres Licht zu stellen, damit
uns kein falscher Tag verführt, was wir begehren sollten zu verabscheuen, und
was wir verabscheuen sollten zu begehren." (PO. 5, 155.   MK. 5, 50.)

an examination of Aristotle's *Poetics*. In an early number of the *Dramaturgy* Lessing had claimed that the fate of those, whose circumstances are nearest to our own, touches us most profoundly, and that the names of kings and princes add pomp and majesty to a play, but in no way render it more moving.[1] The matter is then dealt with at length in Nos. 74–84.

The reappearance of Aristotle as an authority seems at first sight to be a retrograde step ; for Lessing had progressively emancipated himself from unquestioning acceptance of the views of earlier writers, and moreover Aristotle had been so often quoted by the detested French critics that Lessing's respect for him appears surprising. But only for a moment ; for he at once makes it clear that his respect for Aristotle is not based on faith, but on conviction arising from examination—" To be sure I should soon dispose of the prestige of Aristotle, if only I could dispose of his reasons."[2] He does in fact rehabilitate the reputation of Aristotle, as he had that of Simon Lemm, of Horace, of Cardanus and others, by a return to the original text, in the course of which he exposes the false interpretations of the French.

The famous statement that the incidents of tragedy " arouse pity and fear, wherewith to accomplish its purgation of such emotions "[3] forms Lessing's starting-point. What is the nature of this fear and this pity ? Fear (wrongly translated by Corneille as ' terror ') is, according to Lessing, " by no means the fear which is aroused in us for another person by the misfortune about to befall him, but it is the fear which arises for ourselves, through our similarity to the suffering person ; it is the fear that we ourselves may become this pitied object. In a word, this fear is pity transferred to our-

---

[1] 14, Stück.

[2] " zwar mit dem Ansehen des Aristoteles wollte ich bald fertig werden, wenn ich es nur auch mit seinen Gründen zu werden wüsste." 74, Stück. (PO. 5, 309. MK. 5, 246.)

[3] *Poetics*, Chap. 13.

selves."[1] Here is the first vital point in Lessing's. interpretation. Fear and pity cannot be separated as Corneille had separated them, for fear is simply an aspect of pity.

Lessing is so far correct in substituting " fear " for " terror " and in claiming that tragedy must arouse *both* fear and pity. But in sinking the conception of fear in that of pity, he has exceeded the warrant of his original. Aristotle, as Lessing himself observed, was a great saver of words,[2] and he would not have mentioned " fear " as well as " pity," if the former were only an aspect of pity. For Lessing " pity " is the emotion that matters in tragedy, since " fear " is only a term for " pity " applied to oneself. This domination of pity at the expense of fear is inherent in Lessing's age, the tendency of which was to shun the depths of the soul and the profoundest emotions, and to set its store upon humane conduct.. Hence the high valuation of pity as an humane virtue.

According to Lessing then, we must apply to ourselves the pity we feel for the tragic hero. It will be easiest to imagine ourselves in the situation presented on the stage, if the hero of the tragedy is akin to us and his circumstances resemble ours. These conditions are fulfilled by "domestic tragedy," in which the characters are drawn from the every-day life of the present. Lessing himself states that the conditions of Aristotle will be best fulfilled when the poet portrays the tragic hero as of the same stuff as ourselves.[3]

One of Aristotle's best-known pronouncements has now been pressed into the service of " domestic tragedy."

[1] " durchaus nicht die Furcht, welche uns das bevorstehende Übel eines andern für diesen andern erweckt, sondern es ist die Furcht, welche aus unserer Ähnlichkeit mit der leidenden Person für uns selbst entspringt ; es ist die Furcht, dass die Unglücksfälle, die wir über diese verhänget sehen, uns selbst treffen können ; es ist die Furcht, dass wir der bemitleidete Gegenstand selbst werden können. Mit einem Worte : diese Furcht ist das auf uns selbst bezogene Mitleid." 75, Stück. (PO. 5, 313. MK. 5, 251).

[2] 77, Stück. (PO. 5, 321. MK. 5, 260.)

[3] " wenn er ihn mit uns von gleichem Schrot und Korn schildere." 75,. Stück. (PO. 5, 315. MK. 5, 253).

There remains the long-disputed " catharsis," which, according to Aristotle, takes place through the agency of pity and fear. It is here that Lessing's interpretation is least adequate. To begin with Lessing introduces a moral idea, by translating " catharsis " as *Reinigung* purification.

> As this purification consists simply and solely in the transformation of the passions into virtuous qualities, and as with each virtue there is, according to our philosopher, an extreme in either direction, between which the virtue itself is to be found, so tragedy, if it is to transform our pity into virtue, must be able to purify us from the two extremes of pity ; and the same is to be understood of fear.[1]

The effect of tragedy then is to " transform our passions into virtuous qualities," to leave us neither with too much nor with too little pity, but with just that quantity which constitutes a virtue. It is highly improbable that Aristotle ever entertained any such moral notion of tragedy. " Catharsis " is the medical term, purgation, and Aristotle presumably meant by it the release of highly charged emotion, which, if it was not discharged, would endanger the health of the soul. Lessing's opinion that Aristotle's " catharsis " was an ethical idea, was mistaken. Lessing's view implies that virtue may be attained by way of the emotions, whereas Aristotle held that it could only be achieved by the will. As an interpretation of Aristotle, Lessing's conception of tragedy is untenable, although he has certainly corrected some previous errors.

Aristotle, however, was not infallible. Lessing might still be right, even though his views were not those expressed in the *Poetics*. It is clear, however, that Lessing not only minimizes the fear, terror or horror, which, it is generally recognized, all good tragedies

---

[1] " Da . . . diese Reinigung in nichts anders beruhet, als in der Verwandlung der Leidenschaften in tugendhafte Fertigkeiten, bei jeder Tugend aber, nach unserm Philosophen, sich diesseits und jenseits ein Extremum findet, zwischen welchem sie innestehet : so muss die Tragödie, wenn sie unser Mitleid in Tugend verwandeln soll, uns von beiden Extremis des Mitleids zu reinigen vermögend sein ; welches auch von der Furcht zu verstehen." 78, Stück. (PO. 5, 327. MK. 5, 268.)

arouse, but that he claims a moral effect of tragedy which in no way corresponds to experience. Tragedy acts largely on the subconscious plane, and not, as Lessing would have it, through consciousness alone. It is a profound and valuable experience, not an incitement to virtuous conduct.

What Lessing's theory actually does, is to provide a systematic basis for the " domestic tragedy " of his own day. Both the practice and the theory of this kind of tragedy are the products of an age concerned more with the relationships of men one with another, than with the psychology of the individual. Hence the neglect of the unconscious and the avoidance of shattering emotions.

The *Hamburg Dramaturgy* is full of stimulating and interesting observations, expounded in a style which makes it eminently readable, but no system can be deduced from it which will be valid to-day. It is at once a monument to Lessing's penetrative and analytical power and a revelation of his limitations and those of his age. As the final stage of his campaign against French tragedy in Germany and for the adoption of English taste in its stead, it is of the greatest historical importance.

F

CHAPTER VI

THE SCHOLAR AND THE ANTIQUARIAN

1. HORACE AND SOPHOCLES

THE sound classical education, which Lessing had received at Meissen, was of the utmost value to him throughout his life. In an age when classical literature played a very great part in the cultural life of Europe, Lessing was equipped to intervene authoritatively in all controversies and to cope with the many works of learning written in Latin. He had already displayed his powers in the *Vademecum* and in his writings on Plautus.

The controversy with Lange was probably responsible for the studies which produced the *Rehabilitations of Horace* in 1754.[1] In the preface Lessing makes a statement typical of his truth-loving character and of his combative literary career :

I can have no more pleasant occupation than passing in review the names of famous men, investigating their right to immortality, wiping off unmerited stains, and removing the false patches which conceal their weaknesses ; in short, doing in a moral sense everything which he, who is entrusted with the supervision of a picture-gallery, does in a material sense.[2]

We have already seen how ready Lessing was to salve damaged reputations. His ardour in this case was heightened by his enthusiasm for the poetry of Horace.

The *Rehabilitations of Horace* are intended to refute three accusations commonly levelled, not at the works, but at the life of the Roman poet : that he was lascivious, that he was cowardly and that he was an atheist. Lessing's method is the only sound one, of going straight to the original authorities.

[1] *Rettungen des Horaz* ; published in *Schriften*, 3, Teil.
[2] " Ich selbst kann mir keine angenehmre Beschäftigung machen, als die Namen berühmter Männer zu mustern, ihr Recht auf die Ewigkeit zu untersuchen, unverdiente Flecken ihnen abzuwischen, die falschen Verkleisterungen ihrer Schwächen aufzulösen, kurz, alles das im moralischen Verstande zu tun, was derjenige, dem die Aufsicht über einen Bildersaal anvertrauet ist, physisch verrichtet." (PO. 14, 86.)

The accusation of an immoral life rests on a passage of Suetonius and on the internal evidence of Horace's poems. Suetonius stated that Horace is said to have enjoyed his mistresses in a room, the walls of which were covered with mirrors. By the adroit pursuit of clues and acute combination of deductions, fully as enthralling as any detective-story, Lessing arrives at the conclusion now generally accepted, that the sentence is not genuine, but is a later interpolation, referring not to Horatius, but to a certain Hostius. The ignorance of an early editor had led to this confusion. The gradual accumulation of inferences, as one clue after another is successfully followed up, always increasing the certainty of the ultimate result, makes of these few pages one of the most fascinating examples of Lessing's thoroughness, careful procedure, acute perception and brilliant application of wide reading.

The evidence of the poems is of particular interest to Lessing. The great majority of eighteenth-century critics assumed that poetry contained a literal account of events in the poet's life. Lessing pointed out that the incidents and experiences portrayed may be entirely imaginary :

Must he (the poet) have emptied all the glasses and kissed all the girls, he claims to have emptied and kissed ?[1]

In applying this remark to Horace, Lessing was probably right. It is true that his attitude neglects the value of experience in the lyric poet and that, if pushed to extremes, it would, and in the eighteenth century did, reduce poetry to little more than an intellectual parlour game. But it was a salutary reaction to those critics (and they are not by any means confined to Lessing's own day) who treat poetry as the raw-material of biography. With equal justice Lessing condemned French romantic biographies and *vies amoureuses* (popular then as now) in which the slightest allusions in poems were used to

[1] " Muss er denn alle Gläser geleert und alle Mädgens geküsst haben, die er geleert und geküsst zu haben vorgibt ? " (PO. 14, 95.)

erect elaborate stories about the poet's life on the flimsiest foundation.

Lessing now found it easy to refute the other two allegations, which were based on the evidence of the poems alone. As to the accusation of cowardice, the commentators had, in one case,[1] taken a delicate compliment as literal fact, and in the other had not understood the text.[2] The ode[3] in which the editors had discovered a confession of atheism and various subtle philosophical allusions, was

> simply the expression of emotions which he (Horace) had felt on the occasion of an extraordinary thunderstorm, which had suddenly arisen in clear weather.[4]

Lessing's arguments in this essay testify both to his common-sense and to his scholarship. His conclusions, except for some details, are still accepted to-day. His remarks on the nature of experience in poetry give the essay more than antiquarian significance. As on many other occasions he showed that sound scholarship need not avoid the topical and need not be dull.

Six years later Lessing's interest in the Greek theatre led him to begin a work on Sophocles; it remained unfinished and was published in its fragmentary state in 1790, nine years after his death. *The Life of Sophocles* originated in the idea of another rehabilitation; for Bayle had omitted Sophocles from his encyclopaedic *Dictionary*. Lessing adopted Bayle's method, which he had already used in the Letter of 1753, correcting Jöcher's *Gelehrten-Lexikon*. A succinct account of Sophocles' life, occupying two and a half pages, is followed by seventy pages of notes. The result is an unreadable work of learning, lacking any popular appeal. It is a great pity that Lessing never wrote the second part, which was to have been a commentary on the plays.

---

[1] Ode 7. Book 2.   [2] Epistle 2. Book 2.   [3] Ode 34. Book 1.

[4] " nichts als der Ausbruch der Regungen, die er bei einem ausserordentlichen am hellen Himmel plötzlich entstandenen Donnerwetter gefühlt hat." (PO. 14, 116.)

As it is *The Life of Sophocles* is one of Lessing's least interesting works.

2. FABLE AND EPIGRAM

Lessing's treatises on the fable and on the epigram are general studies of these forms of literature, but both have their origin largely in his classical studies. Both are excellent examples of Lessing's method, of its advantages and of its disadvantages.

The *Treatises on the Fable (Abhandlungen über die Fabel)* were published together with Lessing's own fables in 1759. It is typical of Lessing that theory and practice should go hand in hand. His fables are remarkable for their brevity and for their clear moral. They are a return to the conciseness of Aesop, after the expansion evident in La Fontaine and still more in his German imitator, Gellert. The best of Lessing's fables are in prose, another point of difference from his immediate predecessors and of contact with the Aesopic fable.

The return to Aesop, as Lessing conceived him, is likewise the keynote underlying the theoretical treatise. This begins with an important general essay on the nature of the fable, followed by sections dealing with its various aspects. Lessing's method is to clear away misunderstandings and confusions, and then gradually to build up a definition. He begins by giving a brief provisional definition : it is " a fiction, aiming at a certain purpose."[1]   His power of analysis then comes into play ; he divides fables into two categories, (1) " simple " (*einfach*), in which a general truth is derived from a general occurrence, and (2) "compound" (*zusammengesetzt*), in which the general truth, derived as in the simple fable, is then further applied to a particular, real case ; this latter variety is really a sequence of two fables, of which the second is the application of the first. These are the preliminaries. In order to arrive at a more elaborate

---

[1] " eine Erdichtung, die auf einen gewissen Zweck abzielet." (PO. 15, 37.)

definition, Lessing now has recourse to the method, so familiar with him, of seeking out opinions from which he can differ, and of evolving his own views under the stress of contradiction. On this occasion Lessing passes in review the definitions given by de la Motte, Richer, Breitinger and Batteux, and finds them all wanting in varying degrees. Now, having completed his examination of earlier critics, Lessing sums them up in a definition which is an excellent instance of the way in which he proceeds from negative to positive, from destruction to construction : " In the fable *not any truth*, but a general moral proposition, is *not hidden or disguised*, but referred, *not under the allegory of an action*, but to an individual case, so that I do *not merely discover in it some similarities with the moral proposition*, but entirely and clearly recognize the latter in it."[1] Though this monstrous sentence is very far removed from Lessing's normal prose style, it does reveal, in its predominating negativeness, the extent to which opinions which Lessing did not accept enabled him to sharpen his claws before the final task of establishing a positive proposition. As might be expected from its clumsy form, it is only a stepping stone to Lessing's final definition, which runs as follows : " If we refer a general proposition to a particular case, confer reality upon this case, and make of it a story in which one recognizes clearly the general proposition, then this fiction is a fable."[2] The advantages of Lessing's characteristic method are very evident in this essay, where his negative section clears the mind of error and prejudice before he begins to construct on a foundation as secure as he can make it. Noteworthy too is the ability to present

---

[1] " In der Fabel wird *nicht eine jede Wahrheit*, sondern ein allgemeiner moralischer Satz, *nicht unter die Allegorie einer Handlung versteckt oder verkleidet*, sondern auf einen einzeln Fall, so zurückgeführet, dass ich *nicht bloss einige Ähnlichkeiten mit dem moralischen Satze in ihm entdecke*, sondern diesen ganz anschauend darin erkenne." (PO. 15, 57.)

[2] " Wenn wir einen allgemeinen Satz auf einen besondern Fall zurückführen diesem besondern Falle die Wirklichkeit erteilen und eine Geschichte daraus dichten, in welcher man den allgemeinen Satz anschauend erkennt, so heisst, diese Erdichtung eine Fabel." (PO. 15, 62.)

clearly the various steps of his logical process so that the definition seems to grow before our eyes.

Lessing's method in the remaining essays of this work is similar. The second deals with the use of animals in the fable. As Lessing has a very strict eye to the moral purpose of the fable he has a tendency to give more stress to the use of human beings than of the animals favoured by writers whose design is chiefly to amuse. Nevertheless he is far from rejecting the use of animals either in his theory or his practice. Animals have the advantage of not rousing the passions, so that the reader can calmly recognize the moral.

The third essay is concerned with the division of the fable. Its procedure follows that of the first. Lessing's division of fables into (1) reasonable (*vernünftig*), i.e. realistic and (2) moral (in which certain assumptions must be made, for belief), and his subdivision of the latter class into mythical and hyperphysical[1] illustrate one of the defects into which he is often led by his exceptional clarity of mind coupled with the dialectical method, so highly esteemed by his age. This defect is the too sharp and clear-cut division of artistic forms and even occasionally division and subdivision for no other motive than sheer pleasure in a dialectical process.

In his fourth essay Lessing claims that prose is the most suitable form for the fable. And if his assumption that its aim is exclusively didactic is granted, then no one will question that prose is the correct vehicle just as much as it is in text-books and scientific works.

Lessing's great interest in the fable and the particular view he takes of it reveal most clearly the moral attitude to art, so often remarked already.

Twelve years later, in 1771, he published in the new edition of his collected works a somewhat similar essay on the Epigram under the title *Scattered Observations*

---

[1] Mythical fables involve the belief in beings not existing, e.g., gods and goddesses. Hyperphysical fables are those which involve qualities in existing beings which they do not actually possess, e.g., speech in animals.

on the Epigram (Zerstreute Anmerkungen über das Epigramm). This later work shows a keen perception of the qualities necessary in an epigram, but the practical side has undergone a diminution. Lessing is here concerned with theory, rather as a means for understanding and interpretation, than as a basis for present or future writers. He opens with a definition : " The epigram is a poem, in which after the fashion of an actual inscription our attention and curiosity about a single object are first aroused and more or less sustained, and then suddenly satisfied."[1] Both parts, the anticipation and its satisfaction are equally essential. Lessing then discusses and rejects various definitions suggested by other writers—a reversal of his procedure with the fable —and then goes on to discuss various classical epigrammatists. Of these it is above all Martial who secures his approval. According to Lessing, he was the first writer to devote himself exclusively to the epigram and still remains the best.[2] In the course of his appreciation of Martial he displays a very just conception of the function of biography in criticism—" Besides, the true life of a poet is his poems. Only what can be said of these can still have value, and the most important details about an ancient author are only important in so far as they serve to explain his works."[3] He attacks the commentators for their total lack of any fine appreciation of literature and states that in classical literature much remains to be done, " which can only be expounded by taste and sensibility."[4] These are precisely qualities which Lessing himself possessed; together with common sense and

[1] " das Sinngedicht ist ein Gedicht, in welchem nach Art der eigentlichen Aufschrift unsere Aufmerksamkeit und Neugierde auf einen einzeln Gegenstand erregt und mehr oder weniger hingehalten werden, um sie mit eins zu befriedigen." (PO. 14, 121.)

[2] PO. 14, 154-5.

[3] " Dazu sind das wahre Leben eines Dichters seine Gedichte. Nur was von diesen zu sagen ist, das kann allein noch jetzt einen wahren Nutzen haben, und die wichtigsten Nachrichten von einem alten Verfasser sind nur in so weit wichtig, als sie seinen Werken zur Erläuterung dienen können." (PO. 14, 167.)

[4] " was sich in ihnen durch Geschmack und Empfindung erklären lässt." (PO. 14, 182.)

penetrative power, they render his commentaries on ancient authors of interest, even in those cases where later research has invalidated his findings.

3. LAOCOON

Up to the middle of the 'sixties Lessing's works had shown interest in literature alone among the arts.   The appearance therefore of *Laocoon, or On the Limits of Painting and Poetry* (*Laokoon, oder über die Grenzen der Mahlerei und Poesie*) in 1766 was a complete surprise to all except his friends.

The first stimulus to this work had come from Winckelmann's *Thoughts on the Imitation of Greek Works in Painting and Sculpture* (1755) and was considerably augmented by the publication of this same author's *History of the Art of Antiquity* (1764)   The work of Winckelmann is significant as a revival of the study of the plastic arts of the Ancients and laid the foundation of the conception that serenity was the fundamental characteristic of Greek art—a conception which was to hold the field for more than a century, till it was undermined and finally overthrown by Nietzsche.   As is well-known, Winckelmann had written in the earlier work of " a noble simplicity and serene grandeur as well of attitude as of expression," which in his view were typical of Greek art.   Winckelmann's application of these characteristics to literature as well as to sculpture was the starting point of Lessing's work.

A quotation from Winckelmann opens *Laocoon*. After giving the phrase cited above Lessing goes on to quote Winckelmann's verdict on the Laocoon group. This famous sculpture, now in the Vatican, represents Laocoon and his two sons struggling in the coils of the serpent.   It is now generally agreed that it is the work of Rhodian artists about the year 50 B.C. ; the assumption of Lessing that it belongs to the epoch of Titus (*c.* A.D. 70–80)[1] is no longer tenable.   The feature of the group

[1] Section XXVI.

which Winckelmann considered particularly noteworthy
was the half-open mouth of the principal figure.   From
this it was evident that Laocoon was not shrieking.
Winckelmann concluded that he was portrayed as suffering with stoic endurance and that he therefore exhibited
more sublime grandeur of soul in this statue than the
Laocoon of Virgil, who does not repress his shrieks.

Lessing's suspicions were aroused by the unfavourable
mention of Virgil.   This led him first to an examination
of Greek literature which might show that the Greeks
considered shrieks to be the natural and normal expression of pain.   Obvious instances occur at once in
Philoctetes and in *The Women of Trachis*.   The former of
these had even received a word of praise from Winckelmann in the passage dealing with Laocoon.   Lessing
was thus easily able to establish that the screams were no
national peculiarity.   In literature both Greek and
Roman authors let their characters cry out when in pain.
The fact that Laocoon in the statue does not scream must
therefore have some quite different origin from that which
Winckelmann had alleged.

Once more Lessing has set out from a view with which
he disagrees ; and once more he will evolve something
new and constructive out of the contradiction.   In
Laocoon, however, his premises are not as sound as in his
works of literary criticism.   He first postulates that
" beauty was the highest law of art for the ancients "[1] and
then proceeds to set up this law as a binding principle for
his own day.   He also assumes that the aim of painting
and sculpture is pleasure.[2]   In the first of these statements is implied the view that the principles of the plastic
arts are absolute, and consequently applicable to all times
and all races.   The whole of Lessing's argument depends
on the identification of Greek art and literature with the
art and literature of Lessing's own day.

[1] " bei den Alten die Schönheit das höchste Gesetz der bildenden Künste
gewesen sei." Section II. (PO. 4, 300. MK. 4, 29.)

[2] Section II. (PO. 4, 299. MK. 4, 28.)

Working from this basis, Lessing states that the ancients avoided, in painting and sculpture, the presentation of passions which would distort the face and thus render it ugly. The sculptor of the Laocoon group " was working to achieve the highest beauty under the assumed circumstances of the greatest pain. This latter, with all its disfiguring violence, could not be combined with the former. He had therefore to modify it ; he had to soften the shrieking into sighing, not because shrieking betrays an ignoble soul, but because it distorts the features in a disgusting manner."[1] Lessing has now established his view that the expression of Laocoon is modified because the laws of the plastic arts could not otherwise have been fulfilled ; soon this is taken one step further, when he states that, as this modification emanates from reasons which " are all derived from the peculiar nature of art and from its necessary limits and requirements,"[2] these laws are not applicable to poetry. Here at last Lessing reveals his aim. He wishes to establish the different principles governing the plastic arts and literature, principles based on the different media employed.

After criticizing at length and rejecting the opinions of those who had held the identity of method for art and literature, notably Joseph Spence and the Comte de Caylus, Lessing arrives at last at the vital distinction between painting and sculpture on the one hand, and literature on the other.[3] The medium of painting is " figures and colours in space," that of poetry " articulated sounds in time,"[4] and the objects portrayed must

[1] " arbeitete auf die höchste Schönheit, unter den angenommenen Umständen des höchsten Schmerzes. Dieser in aller seiner entstellenden Heftigkeit war mit jener nicht zu verbinden. Er musste ihn also herabsetzen ; er musste Schreien, in Seufzen mildern ; nicht weil das Schreien eine unedle Seele verrät, sondern weil es das Gesicht auf eine ekelhafte Weise verstellet." (PO. 4, 302. MK. 4, 32.)

[2] " allesamt von der eigenen Beschaffenheit der Kunst und von derselben notwendigen Schranken und Bedürfnissen hergenommen sind." Section IV. (PO. 4, 306. MK. 4, 38.)

[3] Section XVI.

[4] " Figuren und Farben in dem Raum . . . artikulierte Töne in der Zeit." (PO. 4, 360.)

necessarily be appropriate to these methods. These appropriate objects are then defined as follows :

Objects which exist adjacent to one another or whose parts exist adjacent to one another are termed bodies. Hence bodies with their visible properties are the true subjects of painting.

Objects which succeed one another or whose parts succeed one another are termed actions. Hence actions are the true subject of poetry.[1]

Painting is limited to a single moment of time and " must therefore choose the most pregnant moment."[2] Neither art may trespass on the subject matter of the other. Descriptive poetry is therefore a contradiction in terms.

Realizing that his verdict narrowed unduly the field of poetry Lessing devoted a good deal of space in the rest of the work to devices by which the poet might convey the effect of physical beauty without describing it. These devices are drawn from the practice of Homer. Gradually Lessing lost sight of his main theme and the final sections no longer have any relevance to it, but consist of miscellaneous observations on Winckelmann's *History of the Art of Antiquity*.

Laocoon, in spite of the interest it excited at the time, is not a satisfactory work. Compared with most of Lessing's writings it is haphazard and without plan. In the preface he admits that it is rather a collection of materials for a book than a book itself, and that many digressions are included because he had no other suitable place for them.

As far as Lessing's observations on plastic art are concerned it is clear that he has ventured into a field where he is no competent judge. His ideas on art bear no relationship to the practice of his own age and are based,

---

[1] " Gegenstände, die nebeneinander oder deren Teile nebeneinander existieren heissen Körper. Folglich sind Körper mit ihren sichtbaren Eigenschaften die eigentlichen Gegenstände der Malerei. Gegenstände, die aufeinander oder deren Teile aufeinander folgen, heissen überhaupt Handlungen. Folglich sind Handlungen der eigentliche Gegenstand der Poesie." (PO. 4, 360. MK. 4, 118.)

[2] " muss daher den prägnantesten (Augenblick) wählen." (PO. 4, 361. MK. 4, 119.)

not on first-hand observation, but on what he had read about Greek sculpture and on references and descriptions in ancient writers, or at best on the examination of engravings of statues, engravings which were very often inaccurate. It seems to us incredible that anyone should attempt an interpretation of the Borghese Gladiator without any closer knowledge of the original than an engraving in which, as it subsequently proved, the position of the right and left legs was transposed.[1] Second-hand knowledge of this kind was obviously dangerous. Such procedure, unfortunately only too common in the eighteenth century, shows how much his approach to the plastic arts was dominated by literature, and this is borne out by many other features of the work. His vital definition seems valid to him because it agrees with the practice of Homer, not from any accordance with works of plastic art. Even in the work which forms the starting-point of the treatise, the Laocoon, lack of first-hand knowledge has led Lessing, as it had led Winckelmann to misunderstand the work, for Laocoon neither shrieks nor sighs, for he is drawing in breath, whilst the expression of pain is, contrary to the assumption of either critic, unmistakably violent in the eyes, the face and the whole muscular frame of the central figure. There was no diminution of the expression of pain in Laocoon, whether from the reason suggested by Lessing or that suggested by Winckelmann. The undue importance given by Lessing to the subject in art is also a result of his excessively literary approach.

Another major defect of *Laocoon* is the absolute standpoint which Lessing assumes. It has already been mentioned that he conceives the procedure of the ancients in the plastic arts as binding for all subsequent ages ; but more than that, he extends this absolute view to literature, regarding the method of Homer as possessing a similar prescriptive value. Lessing's exposition of devices in poetry betrays anew the conscious intellectual attitude to

[1] Section XXVIII. The work is now in the Louvre.

artistic creation, which he had progressively discarded. The work represents therefore a retrograde step in his criticism. This may in part be explained, though not excused, by the fact that the views expressed were largely evolved in discussion with his friend Moses Mendelssohn, a noted exponent of dialectical absolute criticism.

4. ANTIQUARIAN CONTROVERSY

The dogmatic statements of *Laocoon* called forth many attacks, both justified and unjustified. Professor Heyne of Göttingen corrected the mistake Lessing had made over the Borghese Gladiator.[1] But of all those who attacked Lessing's views one of the most persistent was Professor Adolf Klotz. This Klotz, who had already attempted to open a correspondence with Lessing and with whom Lessing had politely differed in *Laocoon*, was unquestionably a superficial scholar.

In 1767 Klotz had founded a periodical, *The German Library of the Fine Arts* in direct rivalry with Nicolai's *Library of the Fine Arts*. In this he sought to make himself an arbiter of taste and opinion in Germany, as Lessing himself had done in his various journalistic activities. The tone of this periodical excited in Lessing nothing but contempt,[2] but the affectation of superiority, which characterized Klotz' references to Lessing in his book on carved gems[3] published in 1768, soon produced another reaction, that of anger. " The man throws his weight about," wrote Lessing to Nicolai, " and would like to pass for an oracle in such things. All the same I am convinced that never has a more ignorant rogue attempted to possess himself of the critical tripod."[4]

---

[1] See *Antiquarian Letters* Nos. 36–7, and letter of 5th January 1769, to Professor Heyne.

[2] See letter to Nicolai, 2nd February 1768.

[3] *Ueber den Nutzen und Gebrauch der alten geschnittenen Steine und ihrer Abdrücke.*

[4] " Der Mann nimmt das Maul gar zu voll, und möchte lieber ein Orakel in solchen Dingen vorstellen. Gleichwohl bin ich gewiss, dass es nie einen unwissendern armen Teufel gegeben, der sich des kritischen Dreifusses bemächtigen wollen." Letter of 9th June, 1768.

Lessing was not the man to abstain long from action and accordingly there appeared on 20th and 22nd June, 1768, in two Hamburg newspapers, a reply to Dusch, one of Lessing's old opponents, rebutting Klotz' allegation that Lessing had been guilty of an " unpardonable error " in *Laocoon*. This reply constitutes the first of the *Letters of Antiquarian Content (Briefe antiquarischen Inhalts)* which Lessing published in 1768 and 1769 and which form the most important part of the campaign against Klotz. They are double-edged ; on the one hand they are a defence of those points in *Laocoon* which Klotz had attacked, whilst on the other hand they contain a violent counter-attack and mercilessly expose the numerous shortcomings, inaccuracies and plagiarisms of Klotz' own book.

Though subsequent generations have rejected many of the judgments of *Laocoon*, Lessing had no difficulty in refuting the objections advanced by Klotz, arising as they did either from the latter's ignorance or from his deliberate failure to understand Lessing's argument. In the second part, it is true, Lessing is obliged to retract his interpretation of the Borghese Gladiator, but even here he succeeds in showing that, though Professor Heyne's objection was justified, his supposition as to the manner in which it occurred was incorrect. As Klotz had repeated this in full as his own, he was therefore exposed even here as a plagiarist.

When Lessing turns to attack Klotz' own book, his bitterness surpasses even that of the *Vademecum for Mr Lange*. Sentence by sentence Lessing demonstrates that Klotz knew nothing of the subject on which he set up to be an authority, but was merely summarizing other writers and even then misunderstanding their sense. Klotz' use of language is loose, his use of terms incorrect. One of his statements " read once, cursorily, it sounds as if it really were something. And it is nothing, nothing but words without sense."[1] To Klotz' personal accusa-

---

[1] " nur einmal, so obenhin gelesen, klingt es wirklich, als ob es etwas wäre. Und es ist nichts, nichts als Worte ohne Sinn." Letter 41. (PO. 17, 195.)

tions he replies with an account of their scanty correspondence, which proves that all the advances came from Klotz' side.   The latter's defamatory, personal mode of criticism should be called *Klotzianism* as a perpetual monument to his infamy.   When Klotz objects that Lessing's style is often more than merely satirical, Lessing retorts, " I am sorry if my style is ever merely satirical.   It is always my intention that it should be more than satirical. And what shall it be that is more than satirical ?   It shall be to the point."[1]   Finally when Klotz complains that Lessing's tone recalls the *Vademecum*, Lessing answers,

> And to whose shame will this forced recollection redound ? To mine ? How can I help it, if his book contains just such childish howlers as Lange's Horace ?[2]

Klotz did not yield so easily to Lessing's crushing invective as Lange had done fifteen years before.   He continued to fulminate against Lessing till his death in 1771, but his prestige was irretrievably ruined by Lessing's exposure, in the final letters, of his calumnies and intrigues.

It is always interesting to discover how an author sees himself.   These letters contain a self-portrait of Lessing in the guise of a mill, against which Klotzian Quixotes tilt in vain :

> I am really a mill and no giant.   There I stand in my place, right outside the village, alone on a sand-hill, and come to nobody and help nobody and demand help from nobody.   When I have something to shake out onto my stones I grind it up with the help of whatever wind is blowing.   All the thirty-two winds are my friends. I do not demand an inch more of the whole wide atmosphere than my sails need to turn round.   But they must be left free to turn round.   Gnats can swarm between them ; but mischievous boys must not always be trying to rush between them ; still less must a hand try to check them which is not stronger than the wind which drives them round.   He whom my sails hurl into the air can blame

---

[1] " Es tut mir leid, wenn mein Stil irgendwo bloss satirisch ist.   Meinem Vorsatze nach, soll er mehr als satirisch sein.   Und was soll er mehr sein als satirisch ? Treffend." Letter 57. (PO. 17, 260.)

[2] " Aber zu wessen Beschämung wird diese erzwungene Erinnerung gereichen ? Zu meiner ? Was kann ich dafür, dass sein Buch ebenso kindische Schnitzer hat als der Langische Horaz ? " (PO. 17, 260.)

himself for it ; nor can I put him down any more gently than he falls.[1]

On the whole Lessing's whimsical description of himself in this passage is fair as well as amusing, though it cannot be denied that his opponents and notably Klotz struck the ground a little harder than they would have through a mere fall.   Certain it is, however, that he did not seek literary quarrels and that those in which he was involved were either stimulated by bad work or by personal provocation.

The *Antiquarian Letters*, tedious and trivial as the subject-matter of them must seem to the general reader, constitute a master-piece of polemics and invective. Their defects are the sophistries with which Lessing defends certain untenable positions[2] and the occasional exaggeration of errors he discovered in Klotz' work.   In extenuation of this latter feature, it may be pointed out that in the two works in which these faults occur (the *Antiquarian Letters* and the *Vademecum*) Lessing was incensed by a base personal attack made upon him by his adversary.

These letters were not the only work which the dispute with Klotz provoked.   An essay *On the Ancestral Portraits of the Ancient Romans* remained unpublished.   Another work, *How the Ancients portrayed Death* (*Wie uie Alten den Tod gebildet*), published in 1769, transforms the purely destructive criticism of the *Antiquarian Letters* into a

---

[1] " Ich bin wahrlich eine Mühle und kein Riese.   Da stehe ich auf meinem Platze, ganz ausser dem Dorfe, auf einem Sandhügel allein und komme niemandem und helfe niemanden und lasse mir von niemanden helfen.   Wenn ich meinen Steinen etwas aufzuschütten habe, so mahle ich es ab, es mag sein, mit welchem Winde es will.   Alle zweiunddreissig Winde sind meine Freunde. Von der ganzen weiten Atmosphäre verlange ich nicht einen Fingerbreit mehr, als gerade meine Flügel zu ihrem Umlauf brauchen.   Nur diesen Umlauf lasse man ihnen frei.   Mücken können dazwischen fahren ; aber mutwillige Buben müssen nicht alle Augenblicke sich darunter durchjagen wollen ; noch weniger muss sie eine Hand hemmen wollen, die nicht stärker ist als der Wind, der mich umtreibt.   Wen meine Flügel mit in die Luft schleudern, der hat es sich selbst zuzuschreiben ; auch kann ich ihn nicht sanfter niedersetzen als er fällt." Letter 55. (PO. 17, 254.)

[2] Letters 13 and 14.

G

positive achievement. In the preface Lessing defends
this continuation of his dispute by pointing out that,
although truth is rarely attained by polemics, they assist
greatly in the discovery of truth by exposing what is
false.

The occasion for this work was a statement by Lessing
in *Laocoon*, that the Ancients did not portray death as a
skeleton.[1] Klotz missed the point entirely and believed
that he had refuted Lessing, when he pointed out that the
ancients certainly portrayed skeletons on carved gems.
Before proceeding to the body of the essay Lessing
stresses the irrelevance of Klotz' remark—" When I say
' it is not yet night,' then Mr. Klotz says, ' but noon is
long past.' When I say, ' seven plus seven does not
make fifteen,' then he says, ' but seven and eight do make
fifteen.' And he calls that contradicting me, refuting
me, pointing out to me unpardonable mistakes ! "[2] As
Lessing goes on to say, he had never questioned the fact
pointed out by Klotz. He had simply claimed that these
skeletons of the ancients did not represent Death.

Basing his argument on various engravings of ancient
sarcophagi, Lessing arrives firstly at the conclusion that
the Greeks portrayed Death as a youth, the brother of
Sleep, and secondly that the skeletons they portrayed
represent, not Death, but larvae or lemures, spectres and
spirits of the departed. More recent research has shown
that Lessing was right in claiming that the ancient Greeks
never depicted Death as a skeleton. His theory that
Death always appeared as a youth and his interpretations
of the sculptured figures on the sarcophagi have not
stood the test of time so well. Inaccurate engravings
and scarcity of material are responsible for this failure.

An important feature is Lessing's constructive applica-

[1] Section X. (PO. 4, 345. MK. 4, 99. Note.)

[2] " Wenn ich sage, ' es ist noch nicht Nacht,' so sagt Herr Klotz, ' aber
Mittag ist doch schon längst vorbei.' Wenn ich sage, ' sieben und sieben macht
nicht funfzehn,' so sagt er, ' aber sieben und achte macht doch funfzehn.' Und
das heisst er, mir widersprechen, mich widerlegen, mir unverzeihliche Irrtümer
zeigen ! " (PO. 17, 313. MK. 6, 74.)

tion of the work to his own age ; for he concludes, as in all his best work, with a practical suggestion. He proposes namely that the sculptors of his own day should adopt this serener portrayal of Death, a suggestion which received the support of Herder and was actually put into practice in sepulchral monuments. " The Scriptures themselves," wrote Lessing, " speak of an angel of death ; and what artist would not rather portray an angel than a skeleton ? "[1]   In spite of the sentimentality into which this practice degenerated in the nineteenth century, Lessing's own attitude to death in this essay is manly and resolute.   His rationalistic attitude does not diminish or shirk the issue—though dying has terrors, being dead is only the longed-for end of these terrors.   The agnostic attitude to an after-life, current in his day, had, as Lessing perceived, deprived the skeletons of all justification as an image of death, though, in prescribing the angel of death as a substitute, his wish to be practical led him to trespass on what should more properly be the domain of the creative artist.

This long and in some ways wearisome controversy had been entirely confined to most specialized and consequently, for the general public, most tedious subject matter.   Yet such was Lessing's ability to give life even to the most unpromising material, by his sense of proportion and his vigorous style, that these works remain most interesting despite their frequent inadequacy in the light of present-day research.   A doubt as to their validity is expressed by Lessing himself in *How the Ancients portrayed Death*, where he speaks of the risk in such studies of building on shifting sands,[2] and this work is in fact the last to be exclusively inspired by antiquarian studies.

[1] " Die Schrift redet selbst von einem Engel des Todes ; und welcher Künstler sollte nicht lieber einen Engel als ein Gerippe bilden wollen ? " (PO. 17, 356. MK. 6, 132.)

[2] PO. 17, 337. MK. 6, 106.

5. Miscellaneous Scholarship

Lessing was interested primarily in the German literature of his day. His attention was first led to the history of German literature in his early twenties by the publication by Bodmer and Breitinger of various medieval poems between 1753 and 1757. His work in this field· was slight ; but the firm hold he had upon the present before he approached the past gave him an advantage over the purely academic scholar.

The first important product of Lessing's interest in literary history was an edition of the seventeenth-century epigrammatist, Friedrich von Logau, published in collaboration with Lessing's friend Ramler. The preface is extravagant in praise of Logau. The text, though superior to that of the only selection then available, suffered many distortions and embellishments, chiefly from the hand of Ramler. The most interesting feature, however, is the glossary which Lessing appended to the edition. His eminently practical mind is at once evident in the preface. Many good German words used by Logau had been allowed to become obsolete and so this collection of the words was to be of service not only to readers but to the writers of Lessing's own day, who might well reintroduce many of Logau's best expressions.[1]

A similar work appeared in 1771, an edition of the work of the seventeenth-century Silesian poet, Andreas Scultetus, this time an original discovery by Lessing.

It was after his appointment as Librarian at Wolfenbüttel, however, that Lessing made his most important contribution to research in this field, *On the so-called Fables of the Time of the Minnesingers (Über die sogenannten Fabeln aus den Zeiten der Minnesinger)*. This was an essay published in 1773 as one of the Contributions *To History and Literature, From the Treasures of the Ducal Library at Wolfenbüttel*. With the aid of a copy he discovered in the Library Lessing was able to demonstrate that a

[1] PO. 16, 235.

German fable-book printed at Bamberg in 1461 was practically identical with the fables published by Bodmer and Breitinger. He further showed that the text of this early edition was superior to the MS. they had used. He was also able to prove convincingly in a second contribution published in 1781 that the author of these fables was not Riedenburg, as Gottsched had asserted, but Hieronymus Boner. His view in this question is still undisputed.

Though this is Lessing's chief contribution to the study of German literature in the Middle Ages, he left many notes and fragmentary essays which betray a striking breadth of reading in this subject and very sound views. He was particularly interested in practical philological questions, such as the changes in the vocabulary of the language and in word usage.

Lessing's appointment as Librarian at Wolfenbüttel carried with it the obligation of exploring the resources of the Library in manuscripts. From these he drew material which he published in the *Contributions*. Some of it was new, whilst some of his supposed discoveries proved to be already known. The greater part of this work is of scant interest to the general reader. Exceptions are formed by the essay on the Monastery of Hirsau and the essay *On the Antiquity of Oil-painting* (*Vom Alter der Ölmalerei*), in which he attacked the claim that painting with oil as a mixing medium was the invention of Jan van Eyck. His positive contributions on this subject are however of little value. The subjects of the other essays cover such varied matters as the discovery of a supposedly lost Turkish Manuscript (Beni-Adam), of a more reliable Italian text of the travels of Marco Polo than the Latin ones used hitherto, of a supposedly lost work of Erasmus Stella, and of documents on the origin of the name Marañon for the River Amazon. In all he demonstrates his remarkable ability for the collation and presentation of his material. But the old verve and enthusiasm are lacking.

6. Conclusion : Lessing, the Critic

Lessing possessed in very high degree most of the qualities essential to a great critic. Not only was his reading enormous in quantity, but it was equally remarkable for the wide range of subjects covered, for the thoroughness and for the power of assimilation which he displayed in the course of it. He possessed, too, an excellent memory and a striking ability to collate facts and passages derived from the most varied sources. This appears in all his criticism but is naturally most impressive in works of scholarship. He had, too, a passion for accuracy, whether in translation, in the use of words or in literary research. It is his own accuracy which lends such conviction to the tone of certainty which characterizes his critical writing. What with many authors might seem inexcusable dogmatism becomes with him inevitable truth. And this certainty had for its vehicle a style, clear, precise and emphatic, which all could understand. Even when the matter is inevitably involved, he almost invariably hits suddenly upon some simple image, which lights the whole obscure problem as brilliantly as if the beam of a searchlight were suddenly switched upon it. The characteristic of these sudden flashes is their common-sense. However abstruse the problem and however extravagant previous writings may have been, Lessing never loses his sense of proportion.

He is of course not without defects and limitations. However great his pains to be accurate, he was bound to err sometimes, and his tone of certainty is then dangerously misleading. His conception of psychology, restricted as it was to consciousness, made him unable fully to understand the process of artistic creation. In so far as this process was unconscious he neglected it, and the main burden of his criticism is concerned less with the way in which works of art come into being than with their effect on the reader or beholder. This is in itself no defect, for the question of the relationship of the work of art to the reader is a most vital one, and should certainly not be neglected.   But preoccupation with this problem, combined with an exclusively conscious psychology, was bound to produce a strictly didactic view of art, and this is Lessing's second great limitation.   However comprehensible this may be, it was bound to affect the validity of many of Lessing's views for later generations. The same bias towards the conscious is responsible for the belief that it is possible to formulate rules for creation deduced from the reaction which the artist must produce in the reader or spectator.   This last point somewhat detracts from the value of Lessing's practical criticism in so far as it attempts to arrive at absolute positions, though his common sense usually preserves him from the worst excesses of absolutist aestheticians.   All these limitations are limitations of his age ; he possessed its virtues in superlative degree and it is small wonder that he also betrayed some of its shortcomings.

Perhaps the most striking feature of Lessing's criticism is its constructive aspect.   He is never content with a negative criticism, but always proposes some practical substitute for what he destroys.   This is noticeable throughout the period of his most valuable critical work, his journalistic criticism between the years 1750 and 1769.   For after his appointment as Librarian at Wolfenbüttel in 1770, his critical activity practically ceased.   His great practical achievement was the rejection of French principles of taste and the substitution for them of English models, whose whole spirit had more affinity to the German mind.   In rendering this vital service he could claim more than any other single man to be the founder of modern German literature.

Part Three

LESSING AS DRAMATIST

CHAPTER VII

DRAMATIC APPRENTICESHIP

To claim that Lessing is a great dramatist would be idle. On his own admission he was no creative writer.[1] Nevertheless a considerable body of his work consists of plays ; and these are not confined to any one period of his life, though it is true that the greater number belong to the early years of his literary activity. As natural talent was not responsible for his interest in and practice of the theatre, it is worth inquiring what can have led him in the first place to devote himself to play-writing.

Various external circumstances certainly played a large part, and among these principally the fact that Leipzig in Lessing's student days could show the most flourishing theatre in Germany. The influence of his friend Mylius, who had already written a comedy in 1745 (*Die Ärzte*) and of Weisse, also played its part. There were, however, three factors which lay deeper. Firstly, the admiration that Lessing cherished for a while in Leipzig for French literature, the greatest achievements of which lay in the sphere of the drama, stimulated in him an interest in the theatre and a respect for it as the most suitable form of expression for the supreme genius. Secondly, he realized that here fame could be most quickly achieved. The third reason is of a higher order. It is characteristic of Lessing that he esteems man above art. In his *Preface to Thomson's Tragedies* (*Vorrede zu Thomsons Trauerspielen*) of 1756 he states that he would rather have created the most monstrous and deformed of men than have made the most beautiful statue of Praxiteles.[2] Now of all forms of art the drama affords the nearest approach to the creation of men, since the raw material of its presentation, that is to say the actor, is man himself. Here lies the secret of the fascination which the

---

[1] *Hamburgische Dramaturgie*, 101–4. (PO. 5, 407.)   [2] PO. 7, 87.

theatre exercised on Lessing not only in his callow Leipzig days, but in his maturest years.

Already in his last years at school Lessing had begun two comedies and from this it is clear that Leipzig only intensified an interest which already existed. The first of these plays, *Damon, or True Friendship* (*Damon, oder die wahre Freundschaft*) was printed in 1747 in Mylius' *Ermunterungen*. It is in one act and deals with the exposure of false friendship. The two friends, Damon and Leander, pay court to a young widow, who declares that she will marry the one who is more fortunate in his affairs. Each has entrusted his fortune to a ship destined for the East Indies. Leander makes many protestations of fidelity to Damon but seeks at the same time to deceive him. The latter's ship is lost and Leander is loud in triumph, which however is short-lived, for the widow wisely bestows her hand on Damon who is more " fortunate " since the disaster has made his upright character evident. This play is no more than a trifle and is even in many respects a poor trifle, so insipid is the widow, so transparent the dishonesty of Leander and so undeveloped the character of Damon. Yet it shows already tendencies which are typical of Lessing in his dramatic work. What was most important to him was evidently the moral idea contained in the play—that true friendship consists not in empty protestation but in actions. Further, against the turpitude of Leander is set the unassuming integrity of Damon so that the condemnation is accompanied by a model of true friendship.

The other comedy, *The Young Scholar* (*Der junge Gelehrte*), was begun at Meissen as early as 1745, when Lessing was only sixteen. It did not receive its final form, however, till 1747. In that year Lessing on one occasion criticized adversely a comedy performed in Leipzig ; when his listeners objected that fault-finding is easy, he countered with the undertaking to write a better comedy. The result of this dispute was the completion of *Der junge*

Gelehrte. The meagre plot of this play turns on the prize offered in 1747 by the Berlin Academy of Sciences for an essay on the theory of monads. Damis, the young scholar, is devoured with conceit over his learning. He awaits the announcement that he has won the prize. To his discomfiture, his dissertation has not even been thought worthy of consideration and all his claims to learning are exposed as groundless. Into this main theme is woven a love episode in the French manner. This latter intrigue is far more complex than the episode of the prize, and the two themes, though they alternate, are not adequately connected one with another. The comic effect of the play arises from the exposure of the foibles of Damis, from the impudence and low cunning of the servants (from whom the action proceeds as so often in French comedy) and from the vulgar mercenary father of Damis. It is always on the surface however, arising simply from the speeches and never truly emanating from a living character. The unreality of these puppets reaches its culmination in Juliane, a monster of virtue, who insists on placing gratitude to Damis' father higher than her love for Valer, even after she has learned the base motive which had prompted the benefits she had received. In spite of the mediocrity of the play there is some originality in the figure of Damis, marionette though he is. The young pedant was a type which Lessing knew at first hand. "As I had grown up among this vermin was it any wonder that I should turn my first satirical weapons against it ? " he says in the preface to that volume of his *Writings* which contained this play.[1] It is this satire against the shallow abuse of logic and false pretentions of learning which constitutes the only value which *The Young Scholar* still possesses. Consider the following reductio ad absurdum :

Damis : Eat ? In the strictest sense you can't do that either.
Anton : I ? I can't eat ? Nor drink either, probably ?

[1] " Unter diesem Ungeziefer aufgewachsen, war es ein Wunder, dass ich meine ersten satirischen Waffen wider dasselbe wandte ? " (*Schriften,* 1754. Vorrede III and IV Band. PO. 7, 41.)

Damis : You can eat, that is to say you can cut up your meat, place it in your mouth, chew it, swallow it and so on. But at the same time you cannot eat, that is to say, you do not know the physical laws according to which all this takes place ; you do not know the function of each muscle which is therein active. . . .[1]

In the same vein Lessing ridicules the current prejudice against German achievement in the intellectual field, a prejudice shared even by Frederick the Great :

Damis : I have long been weary of staying in Germany, this Northern seat of rudeness and stupidity, where every element hinders one from being intelligent, where scarcely one mind like mine is born in a century.

Chrysander : Have you forgotten that Germany is your fatherland ?

Damis : Fatherland be hanged !

Chrysander : You scoundrel, why not say straight out, Your father be hanged ![2]

The Young Scholar certainly shows already the influence of Lessing's frequent visits to the Leipzig theatre. Its completion was not indeed his first dramatic work in Leipzig. Already in collaboration with Weisse he had carried out a translation of Marivaux' *Annibal* (1720) in rhyming alexandrines, with the object of securing free passes for the theatre, his finances being already at a low ebb. The director of this theatre, then the most famous in Germany, was Johann Neuber, but the real driving force was his wife, Friederike Caroline Neuber. This talented actress had schooled herself in the French style of declamation and was therefore very ready to identify

---

[1] *Damis :* Essen ? Je nun, wahrhaftig, wenn ich es genau nehmen will, so kannst du es auch nicht.
Anton : Ich ? ich nicht essen ? Und trinken wohl auch nicht ?
Damis : Du kannst essen, das ist : du kannst die Speisen zerschneiden, in Mund stecken, kauen, herunterschlucken und so weiter. Du kannst nicht essen, das ist : du weisst die mechanischen Gesetze nicht, nach welchen es geschiehet ; du weisst nicht, welches das Amt einer jeden dabei thätigen Muskel ist. . . . (PO. 3, 48.)
[2] *Damis :* Ich bin es längst überdrüssig gewesen, länger in Deutschland zu bleiben, in diesem nordischen Sitze der Grobheit und Dummheit, wo alle Elemente es verwehren, klug zu sein, wo kaum alle hundert Jahr ein Geist meinesgleichen geboren wird. . . .
Chris : Hast du vergessen, dass Deutschland dein Vaterland ist ?
Damis : Was Vaterland ?
Chrys : Du Bösewicht, sprich doch lieber gar : was Vater ! (PO. 3, 117.)

herself with Gottsched's campaign to model the German theatre on French lines. Although Frau Neuber had quarrelled with Gottsched, who was the self-appointed director of German intellectual life, her artistic policy remained unchanged, so that the theatre which Lessing visited so assiduously in 1746–7 was entirely French in spirit. Corneille, Racine and Voltaire for tragedy, Molière and Destouches for comedy, were the models on which the German plays here presented were based, while translations from the French actually outnumbered the native products. It is therefore not surprising to find that Lessing followed up *Hannibal* with an attempt at an original tragedy on French lines. This was *Giangir or the Spurned Throne* (*Giangir oder der Verschmähte Thron*), the manuscript of which is dated 17th April, 1747. Emulation and not inspiration was the incentive for this fragment of 110 lines, which Lessing intended to surpass Weisse's *Mustafa und Giangir*, written shortly before. He was passing through a phase familiar in talented young men, a phase when the desire to achieve fame and to dazzle the world outruns his power of expression, when fragment succeeds fragment and plan succeeds plan, while few works reach completion and none seems to have arisen from inner necessity. Yet though he wrote far too much at this time, Lessing at nineteen was already a firm and independent character, so that almost every project is in some way worthy of interest. So in *Giangir* the play opens with a meeting of the principal characters, without the intervention of the confidants so characteristic of French tragedy, while real skill appears in the heroine's calculated simulation of magnanimity. In the verse too Lessing shows independence, for though he uses the alexandrine, it is unrhymed.

These brief essays in the field of tragedy proved sterile and Lessing soon reverted to comedy. *The Misogynist* (*Der Misogyn*), written in one act in 1748 and published in the *Schriften* of 1755, was later revised and divided into three acts (1767), but the character of the work remained unchanged. The original stimulus was provided by the title of a lost play of Menander. Literary incentives of this kind are common at all times as motives for plays with Lessing, but commonest of all in this early phase. He was then a young man with little experience, with wide reading, with a consciousness of his powers and a great desire to emulate the greatest masters of literature. That he falls woefully short of his ambition is the inevitable consequence of the nature of his analytical rather than creative talent.

The Misogynist is an entirely conventional comedy. The theme is a love-tangle between two pairs of lovers and the humour of the play is dependent entirely on Wumshäter, who is the father of two of the lovers, Laura and Valer. Wumshäter is a fanatical misogynist and opposes the desire of his son and daughter to marry. His resistance is at last overcome in each case, principally by the action of Hilaria, Valer's beloved, who wins his confidence while disguised in man's clothing. The formula, as in the majority of these pseudo-French comedies, consists of an amorous intrigue ending happily with marriage, to which is added a comic character who is more or less incidental to the plot. In one respect *The Misogynist* is worthy of note. The heroine, Hilaria, masquerading as Lelio, far from being passive like most of the women in French comedies, is the most active character of the play and has a will of her own and independence of character. She does not hesitate to assert herself against her somewhat shadowy and ineffectual lover :

> You mustn't always be saying " You must." My good Valerius, you promise to be a rather imperious husband. Kindly allow me the pleasure of finishing the part I have begun as I think fit.[1]

Der Misogyn was certainly a meagre comedy, but it

---

[1] " Sie müssen nicht immer sagen : Sie müssen.—Nein, mein guter Valer, Sie versprechen ein ziemlich gebieterischer Ehemann. Gönnen Sie mir doch immer die Lust, die angefangene Rolle nach meinem Gutdünken auszuspielen." (PO. 3, 131.)

stands head and shoulders above the next work Lessing wrote, *The Old Maid* (*Die alte Jungfer*), published in 1749, but omitted, and rightly so, from the collected works issued in 1754 and 1755. *Die alte Jungfer* bears every sign of hack-work of the worst order. A spinster of fifty possessed with considerable means is wooed by a disreputable retired captain. Her dissipated nephew opposes the match which would deprive him of his inheritance and (temporary) financial salvation. The problem is resolved by the captain agreeing with the nephew to share the spoils. The morality of this play in which roguery is rewarded and patted on the back into the bargain is most untypical of Lessing. Every character is despicable and most are dishonest. The comedy relies upon the most heavy-handed effects— obvious impersonation, crude contrast of words and deeds, while in the first scene occurs an obscene joke, which is a rarity with Lessing. In short, a less typical work cannot be found and the explanation is doubtless to be found in the necessity of raising some money after his financial catastrophe in Leipzig in 1748, a supposition made more likely by the fact that it was rushed into print the very year in which it was written.

The necessity of earning his bread and butter did not however absorb the whole of Lessing's time nor any great part of his energies and this same year of 1749 saw in fact the creation of one of his most interesting dramatic works, the fragment of a tragedy called *Samuel Henzi*. In this work, of which the first act and a part of the second were completed, he treated a theme of white-hot actuality. In the previous year a conspiracy in Berne had ended with the execution of its leader, the Henzi whom Lessing makes the hero of his tragedy. The Senate of Berne rules despotically in the play, and Henzi is the chief mover in a plot to overthrow its tyrannical sway. His revolt is stimulated solely by patriotic motives. He would be perfectly willing to accept the present government if it would rule justly :

H

So would to God the Senate would even now listen to us . . . it is not usurped power that makes a ruler great, but ruling a free people by its free choice.[1]

In his honesty, his moderation and his unselfishness, Henzi stands out in sharp relief from the bloodthirsty, unscrupulous demagogue, Dücret, who foments the revolt from motives of personal vengeance. The fragment which Lessing wrote unfolds the political plot and the characters of Henzi and Dücret and proceeds as far as the successful settlement of a threatened dissension among the conspirators. The work was published in the 22nd and 23rd of the critical *Letters* of 1753,[2] and in the first of these Lessing gave some indication of his plan for the development of the play. The discovery of the plot would have taken place towards the end of the third act and the characters of the various members of the Senate would then have been developed.[3] Lessing states that he conceives Henzi as a true patriot, Dücret as the agitator, Steiger (only mentioned in the fragment) as the true and just head of the state and the other senators as the oppressors. This symmetrical grouping of contrasting pairs is indicative of Lessing's rationalistic, uninspired approach to the work, but it does not diminish its interest. Externally *Samuel Henzi* follows the pattern of French classical tragedy, for its verse is the rhyming alexandrine (at that time the current metre for tragedy in Germany) and Lessing intended to adhere strictly to the three unities. In the twenty-second Letter, in which the first act was published, he makes an interesting reference to this observance of the unities. He admits that " certain great minds " (alluding to Shakespeare) would not have troubled to observe them, but that " we

[1] " Drum wollte Gott, der Rat vernähm' uns heute noch—

. . . .

Dass er ein freies Volk durch freie Wahl regieret.
Dies macht Regenten gross, kein angemasstes Recht."
                              (ll. 165-9. PO. 8, 159-60.)

[2] *Briefe*, 1753.

[3] PO. 8, 165. MK. 3, 228.

beginners " in Germany must obey the rules.[1] Yet
though in these respects he is conventional, in others he
is startlingly original. Above all, the striking actuality of
the subject forces itself upon the reader. The play was
written before the newspaper accounts of the conspiracy
had faded from the minds of the reading public.[2] Johst's
Schlageter[3] is no more topical than this. Even bolder is
the attempt to write a political tragedy which shall
eschew entirely the sentimental interest inseparable from
French classical tragedy. No woman character is so
much as mentioned in the fragment or in Lessing's plan.
As might be expected from such an intention, the value
of the play is primarily in the ideas it contains. Lessing's
awareness of political questions, though in no way
suggested in his previous work, comes as no surprise
when one considers the power and independence of his
mind. Through the mouth of Henzi he attacks the
tyrannical abuse of power in no uncertain terms,[4] but he
is not content with mere destructive criticism. The
same character states positively in what true liberty
consists, emphasizing rationalistic tolerance and
republicanism :

Equally shared care for the common weal, . . . the honest and
unforced assurance that one may follow the truth of which one is
convinced oneself, not that which the priest claims to perceive
for us, just application of the law when poor citizens plead, free
choice of unimportant fashion and customs, untarnished toil which
wins the pleasure of a reward instead of nourishing the lazy bellies
of the great, the sweet duty of fighting for one's fatherland rather
than for the quarrelsome vanity of a king, who would rather a
thousand citizens perished by the sword than miss a single word from

[1] PO. 8, 164. MK. 3, 227.

[2] July 1749.

[3] 1933.

[4] " Allein, wann Eigennutz, den kühnen Rat belebt,
Und wann den Grund des Staats die Herrschsucht untergräbt ;
Wann, die das Volk gewählt zu seiner Freiheit Stützen,
Den anvertrauten Rang gleich strengen Zeptern nützen ;
Wann Freundschaft statt Verdienst, wann Blut für Würde gilt ;
Wann der gemeine Schatz des Geizes Beutel füllt."
(ll. 81–9. PO. 8, 157.)

his title, this, my friends, alone constitutes the dear essence of liberty, in defence of which many a hero has joyfully chosen to die.[1]

In these words are embodied the ideals based on rationalistic thought which characterize most of the thinkers of the earlier part of the eighteenth century, and with Lessing are always allied to his sound common sense, which secures them from exaggeration.

In this choice of subject and in the political rather than psychological treatment, there is a new and striking departure, which stamps the play as unique in spite of the analytical construction on the French model and of the heavy-handed verse. It would seem from Lessing's failure to finish the work that the time was not yet ripe for this new form of drama, which does not in fact find its fulfilment until the *Sturm und Drang* twenty-five years later.

This political phase in Lessing's development is also marked by the plan of a play entitled *The Deliverance of Rome (Das befreite Rom)*, the central episode of which was the revolt against Tarquin after the rape of Lucrece. The republican ideal and the revolt against tyranny were thus the themes of this play as of *Henzi*. The project for *The Deliverance of Rome*, however, differs from the *Henzi* fragment in two important particulars. In taking a remote period of history it was less original than *Henzi*, but the projected crowd scenes are a striking innovation and point clearly to the influence of *Julius Caesar*, which Lessing had been studying at this time. After this brief

---

[1] " Nur gleichgeteilte Sorg' um das gemeine Heil,
  Nur fromme Sicherheit, rechtschaffen ungezwungen,
      .   .   .   .
  Der Wahrheit, die man fühlt, nicht die der Priester sehn
  Und für uns sehen will, freimütig nachzugehn,
  Nur unverfälschtes Recht, wenn ärmre Bürger bitten,
  Nur unbeschimpfte Müh', die nicht statt Lohns Génuss
  Der Grossen faulen Bauch mit sich ernähren muss,
  Nur schmeichelhafte Pflicht, fur's Vaterland zu streiten,
  Statt eines Königes herrschsücht' gen Eitelkeiten,
  Um die ein rasend Schwert eh tausend Bürger frisst,
  Als er ein einzig Wort in seinem Titel misst :
  Nur dieses, Freunde, macht der Freiheit schätzbar Wesen,
  Für die schon mancher Held den süssen Tod erlesen."
                                  (ll. 458–472. PO. 8, 170.)

ebullition his political interest secures no further expression in his work for some years, but the occasional recrudescence of political and social themes from 1759 onwards indicates that it was no mere passing phase.

From farcical comedy Lessing had turned to tragedy, but his projects in this field remained unfinished. He doubtless surmised that the political themes which interested him at that time would have but an indifferent welcome on the stage of his day. He now returned to comedy, not to the farce of *The Old Maid*, but to the didactic style of *The Young Scholar*. His next essay, *The Freethinker (Der Freigeist)* written in 1748, was however a great advance upon his first. As in *The Young Scholar* the love-intrigue is incidental in so far as it is not the main centre of interest for him. Yet in this play he has succeeded in giving it a relationship to the actual character of the principal persons and so has bound it to the intellectual content in a way which renders inapplicable to this work the objection made to the earlier play. *The Freethinker* is constructed on the plot of an unpublished French play by de l'Isle, as Lessing himself candidly admits.[1] From this earlier play came the theme of the two sisters betrothed at their father's wish and each actually in love with her sister's fiancé, as also the solution of the problem by an exchange. But Lessing has added an entirely new and original element by making one of the lovers a cleric and the other a freethinker. The interplay of these two characters became for him the interesting and essential part of the comedy. It is Lessing's intention to pillory the anti-clerical and anti-Christian prejudice then current among advanced thinkers. For this reason Theophan, the cleric, is just, kind and considerate in action as well as words. Bitterly opposed to him is the freethinker, Adrast, harsh, suspicious and of doubtful probity. Lessing loses no time in stating the conflict between these two, for the curtain rises upon them as they argue the merits of their respective

[1] *Theatralische Bibliothek, XIV.* (PO. 12, 430. Note 1.)

opinions. Theophan states the orthodox view of
the freethinker : " Call him what you will, freethinker, a
powerful mind, a deist ; or even, if you are determined to
abuse a more worthy designation, call him a philosopher ;
he remains a monster, a disgrace to mankind,"[1] and he
alleges that Adrast's motive is simply vanity, simply
desire to attract attention to himself. Adrast replies by
twisting these remarks into the terms used by the
narrow-minded members of the clergy, for whom freethinker is synonymous with the depth of moral degrada-
tion. Adrast is clearly transferring his own fault of
narrow prejudice to his opponent, for when left alone he
exclaims, " What man of your cloth is not a hypocrite?"[2]
Nevertheless Adrast is far from being a despicable
character. His suspicion and prejudice is motivated by
the persecution he has suffered : " I have to thank priests
for my misfortune. In spite of the close ties of blood
which bound them to me, they have oppressed me,
persecuted me;"[3] and in an interview with his servant,
Johann, the honesty of his convictions is made evident
by contrast, for Johann believes in free thought as long
as it absolves him from moral obligations and cannot
understand Adrast's adherence to a promise he has given.[4]
It is true that Adrast cannot be acquitted of all double-
dealing. He is already in flight from one creditor, he
attempts to deceive another, and though he does not
love Henriette, he proposes to marry her merely in order
to extricate himself from his financial tangle. Yet
Theophan himself affirms his fundamental goodness :
" Your own heart is my guarantee, your own heart,

[1] *Theophan :* Nennen Sie es, wie Sie wollen : Freidenker, starker Geist
Deist ; ja, wenn Sie ehrwürdige Benennungen missbrauchen wollen, nennen
Sie es Philosoph ; es ist ein Ungeheuer, es ist die Schande der Menschheit.
(PO. 3, 228.)

[2] *Adrast :* Welcher von euch Schwarzröcken wäre auch kein Heuchler ?
(PO. 3, 231.)

[3] *Adrast :* Priestern habe ich mein Unglück zu danken. Sie haben mich
gedrückt, verfolgt, so nahe sie auch das Blut mit mir verbunden hatte. (PO.
3, 231.)

[4] Act I, sc. v. (PO. 3, 235-8.)

Adrast, which is infinitely better than your mind, enamoured of certain pretentious opinions, would wish."[1] His faults are limited to his bitterness and prejudiced blindness and these are in all conscience grave enough. All Theophan's kindness and generosity seems hypocrisy to Adrast and it is only when the outraged Theophan at last loses all patience and denounces Adrast for what he is, that the latter at last realizes Theophan's sincerity. Yet in spite of his anger Theophan's judgment is just and provides the best commentary upon Adrast. Juliane's love, he says, " was attached to a man who was as unworthy of it as he is unworthy to have a friend. Adrast would long ago have realized his success with her, if he were calm enough to see clearly. He sees everything superficially and through the tinted glass of his own preconceived opinions, and would often rather deny the evidence of his senses than abandon his delusion."[2] This outburst, which the reader of the play will agree to be long overdue, does have the desired effect of at once easing the situation between the lovers and of curing Adrast. The blind prejudice of the freethinker has been vanquished by the forbearance and magnanimity of a truly noble orthodox Christian, and with that the didactic intention of the play has achieved its fulfilment. The very nature of the character of Adrast involved a more complex and less conscious psychology than has been remarked in the previous plays. Nor is this confined only to Adrast ; the two women are also more subtly conceived, as each is endeavouring to conceal from herself the true direction of her love. The vivacity and kindness of Henriette makes her infinitely more pleasing

---

[1] *Theophan :* Ihr eigen Herz ist mir Bürge ; Ihr eigen Herz, Adrast, welches unendlich besser ist, als es Ihr Witz, der sich in gewisse gross scheinende Meinungen verliebt hat, vielleicht wünschet. (PO. 3, 228.)

[2] *Theophan :* Diese ging auf einen Mann, der ihrer ebenso unwürdig ist, als unwürdig er ist, einen Freund zu haben. Adrast würde sein Glück in ihren Augen längst gewahr geworden sein, wenn Adrast gelassen genug wäre, richtige Blicke zu tun. Er betrachtet alles durch das gefärbte Glas seiner vorgefassten Meinungen und alles obenhin, und würde wohl oft lieber seine Sinne verleugnen als seinen Wahn aufgeben. (PO. 3, 282.)

than her more pious sister and Lessing has in her created
a character of more than usual reality. The dialogue is
the weakest feature of the play. Its method is too often
dialectical, the characters arguing and each expressing
his point of view in full before the other continues.
Normally the duologue is preferred, as it is obviously
easier to conduct an argument between two persons than
between three. When three or more persons do con-
verse it is generally for comic effect, but it has to be
admitted that the comic element in this play is on a rather
low level. As so often in the plays of the time it emanates almost entirely from the conventionalized servants
derived from French comedy. Yet with all its faults
The Freethinker is at once the most original, the most
living and the most profound comedy Lessing had so far
written.

The interest in questions of faith, which Lessing had
displayed in this last work, appeared in a more obvious
and immediate form in *The Jews* (*Die Juden*), a one-act
play written in the same year, 1749, and published in the
collected edition of 1754. Though *The Freethinker* had
championed an orthodox cleric against a sceptic, it had
been the sceptic's prejudices and not his doubts which
were at issue. In fact the sceptic had been attacked in so
far as he was *unreasonable*. In *The Jews* the prejudice of
the Christian against the Jew is denounced, for that, too,
is unreasonable. This rational cast of mind leads Lessing
in this play to become an advocate of tolerance in matters
of faith, even more clearly than it does in *The Freethinker*,
for he now supports the unpopular unorthodox view.
Anti-semitism was as rife in Lessing's time as it is to-day,
though it was less militant, as the Jews had not then
obtained the share in communal life which they achieved
after their emancipation in the nineteenth century.

Lessing's essay attacking this flagrant injustice took
the form of a play because the dramatic form commanded
the widest public and moreover brought its characters
and its moral home to the audience in a more striking

manner than any other form. It is interesting to note that *The Jews* is an apologia for such noteworthy and exceptional examples of the race as Mendelssohn, rather than a plea for the race as a whole. Its thesis is, in fact, that noble and honest characters may be found among the Jews, just as rogues and scoundrels occur among Christians. This limitation of the scope of the play becomes apparent in the chief character, known simply as " The Stranger " (*Der Fremde*), a Jew, in whom magnanimity, generosity and forbearance occur in a degree remarkable in either Jew or Christian (Aryans were not yet invented). The plot of the play is made as simple as possible in order to facilitate the appreciation of the moral. A Baron with strong anti-semitic prejudices is attacked by robbers near his home and would have perished but for the courageous intervention of an unknown traveller. The Baron attributes the attack to Jews. In his gratitude to his rescuer he offers him the hand of his daughter. The traveller (The Stranger) first exposes the criminals, who are the Baron's own Christian servants, and then reveals himself as a Jew. The Baron promises to amend his opinions of the Jews in future ; meanwhile the marriage question is tacitly dropped. Though the play purports to be a comedy, the comic element is undeniably weak, consisting simply in the exposure of the two rogues through the weakness of one of them for feminine company. Lessing's interest is clearly centred on the serious aspects of the play. The moral is pointed not only by the action, but is also underlined by frequent passages of dialogue. In the third scene the Stranger remarks of the scoundrelly Christian Steward, " This fellow, however stupid he may be or pretends to be, is perhaps a more wicked rogue than has ever been found among the Jews. If a Jew swindles, seven times out of nine the Christian has driven him to it "[1] ; and in his

---

[1] " Vielleicht ist dieser Kerl, so dumm er ist oder sich stellt, ein boshafterer Schelm, als je einer unter den Juden gewesen ist. Wenn ein Jude betrügt, so hat ihn, unter neun malen, der Christ vielleicht siebenmal dazu genötiget." (PO. 3, 199.)

mouth is laid a general statement of the lesson of the
play : " I am no friend of general judgments on whole
peoples. . . . I rather believe that good and evil souls may
occur among all nations."[1]

The defect of *The Jews* is one common to propagandist
plays of all periods ; Lessing is so fired with indignation
and with reforming ardour, that he has subordinated the
artistic necessities of a probable plot and credible,
convincing characters to his didactic aim.   On the one
hand the plot errs on the side of slightness and inadequate
motivation, on the other no character is fully developed
except for the Stranger ; and in the treatment of this
character Lessing has in his ardour defeated his aim by
exaggeration.   It has already been suggested that he is
too exceptional to be accounted a typical figure of any
race, but more than that he is a character of such moral
perfection that he becomes himself incredible.   *The
Jews* is an important landmark in the development of
Lessing's ideas, but as an artistic embodiment of those
ideas it is inferior to *The Freethinker*.

Two other comedies of this period deserve no more
than a casual mention.   These are *The Treasure* (*Der
Schatz*) a one-act comedy written in Berlin in 1749 or
1750, and *Women will be Women* (*Weiber sind Weiber*), one
and a half acts of a comedy which should have extended
to five.   Both of these are imitations of comedies of
Plautus, the first of the *Trinummus* and *Women will be
Women* of the *Stichus*.   Their main features are conventional characterization, and a rather realistic dialogue,
contrasting sharply with a fantastic and improbable plot.
Such a succession of extraordinary coincidences and
unexpected recognitions requires the creation of a world
of fantasy if it is to receive poetic belief.   Both these
plays together with the first sketch for *The Matron of
Ephesus*[2] belong to a period when Lessing was intensely

---

[1] " Ich bin kein Freund allgemeiner Urteile über ganze Völker.—Ich sollte
glauben, dass es unter allen Nationen gute und böse Seelen geben könnte."
(PO. 3, 204.)

[2] Recast at Hamburg, but left unfinished.

interested in the comedies of Plautus. As usual he felt impelled to make some concrete positive contribution over and above his purely critical work, and this took the form of these adaptations from the Latin dramatist. In his enthusiasm Lessing did not fully realize at first that the audience of his day required something totally different from Plautine comedy, where the plot is clearly secondary to the comic and often vulgar speech of the lower-class characters. The process of refinement, to which he subjected these plays in the course of adaptation, deprived them of their characteristic merit.

By 1750 Lessing, at the age of twenty-one, was already the author of seven complete plays, several of which had been performed. Yet, in spite of this apparent success on the threshold of his career, he was to write only five more plays in the remaining thirty-one years of his life. The inference is that he was far from being a born dramatist and this fact is made amply clear by an examination of the various fragments of plays which he wrote during these years of apprenticeship, and which were discovered among his papers after his death. To the true dramatist the characters are created in the mind, at once complete and living, as Minerva rises in full panoply from the head of Jupiter. Lessing's method is a different one. He begins with a bare theme from which he proposes to construct his play, conceives his characters first as types and then afterwards attempts to add the flesh, the heart and life to these bare bones. So it is in the two versions of *The Matron of Ephesus*, in which the second attempts to give life to the general indications and dry scraps of dialogue in the first. So in *The Father an Ape, the Son a Conceited Ass (Der Vater ein Affe, der Sohn ein Geck)*[1] he begins with a single foible and then tries to make from this a living character. Far too often he attempts to supplement this inability to create living beings by lifting

---

[1] Sketch for and fragment of a five-act comedy. (PO. 10, 151.)

whole characters from foreign plays, notably English.[1]
Though Lessing is thus a deliberate thinker, rather than
an instinctive creator, it must be conceded that few
persons lacking the dramatist's fundamental gift have
written better plays.   He has done all that could be done
with the method that was natural to his particular mind.

---

[1] From Wycherley's *Country Wife* in *Der Leichtgläubige*, from Congreve's *Double Dealer* in *Der gute Mann*, etc.

CHAPTER VIII

EXPERIMENTS IN NEW FORMS

1. Miss Sara Sampson

LESSING had now realized that his real talent lay in the field of criticism and of thought, and henceforward his plays are in a sense products of his criticism or of his philosophical work. Their justification lies either in their ability to serve as models, to demonstrate a new path for the drama, or in their intellectual content. And so it is in his critical researches that the genesis of *Miss Sara Sampson* is to be found.

In the first essay of the *Theatralische Bibliothek*,[1] Lessing had drawn attention to certain changes in contemporary drama, one of which was the evolution of a new type of tragedy in England, the characteristic of which was that its persons were taken from the middle-classes. To this new form Lessing gave the name of " domestic tragedy " (*bürgerliches Trauerspiel*). In the following year he determined to give practical expression to his approval of this new departure by writing such a play, thus providing a model and an incentive to German dramatists.

Miss Sara Sampson was written at Potsdam in 1755 and successfully performed at Frankfort-on-the-Oder on 10th July in the same year. The English origin of the play is evident not only in the form but in the setting and characters also. Lessing had in fact an English model in mind, *The London Merchant* of George Lillo (1731), which had obtained some considerable fame in Germany. Lessing's characters purport to be typical English men and women of the upper middle classes. They certainly bear a strong resemblance to the characters of the contemporary novels of Richardson, which were presumed in Germany to give an accurate image of life in England. The spectators recognized the world of these

[1] *Abhandlungen von dem weinerlichen oder rührenden Lustspiele.* (PO. 12, 117.)

popular novels on the stage and this doubtless contributed to some extent to its success.

The theme of the tragedy is an elopement. Mellefont and Sara, the escaping couple, have arrived at an inn. Mellefont, however, defers the marriage ceremony in spite of Sara's pleadings. Meanwhile his former mistress, Marwood, secures an interview with Sara and poisons her. Sara's father arrives, all forgiveness, in time to witness her death. Mellefont then stabs himself over the corpse and the tragedy ends.

By a great effort Lessing has concentrated the events of the play so that the unities of time and place are almost completely observed. The scene opens in the inn very early in the morning, so that the characters, by being up and about betimes, will have some reasonable chance of getting through the various incidents within the limits of one day. And this is certainly accomplished without any striking improbability. The unity of place is another matter. For Lessing's purpose, it was necessary that Sara's father, Sir William Sampson, should arrive and be ready to forgive her before Mellefont's interview with Marwood. But Lessing further wishes to show him to the audience and yet to keep him separated from Sara, for had they met, the play would at once have been at an end and there would have been no tragedy. If he had not felt constrained to avoid changes of scene as far as possible, Lessing could have shown him at first in a neighbouring town, a few miles off. However, the unity of place was still valid for him and consequently the spectator is baffled by the strange scruple which forbids Sir William, while residing in the same inn, for hours on end from hastening into an adjoining room to be reunited with his beloved Sara. In the *Hamburg Dramaturgy* Lessing quotes a remark that characters of tragedies often die of nothing but " the fifth act "[1]; Sara and Sir William are kept apart by the " first act," for no separation, no play. Lessing has sought to diminish

[1] 2, Stück. (PO. 5, 32. MK. 4, 344.)

this improbability by stressing the father's desire to obtain his daughter's forgiveness for his earlier lack of sympathy before he approaches her, but this device has only the effect of rendering Sir William's character less plausible.

None of the characters of *Miss Sara Sampson* is constructed on the grand scale usually associated with tragedy. This is of course a natural feature of " domestic tragedy " which must have as its setting the humdrum middle-class home, and which takes as its sphere the restricted and sentimental emotional life of such an environment. The anonymous Elizabethan play, *Arden of Feversham*, had proved that grandeur could be achieved in a petty environment by the presentation of monstrous crime. The eighteenth century, however, was too cramped by a strict code of morality, by a narrow rationalistic outlook and by an enervating regard for mental as well as physical comfort, to suffer any murder among middle-class characters on the stage, unless it were considerably diluted with several gallons of sentimental tears and flavoured with a large dose of the tender passion. Lessing himself was constantly agitating against this limitation of the dramatist's sphere, which he attributed principally to the influence of French taste, though it is beyond question that its root lay much deeper in the German middle-classes themselves.

Be that as it may, he has here created a typical sentimental heroine. Sara's most salient qualities are that she is kind and virtuous. Her virtue is for Lessing one of the great problems of the play. He found it necessary to lay very heavy stress upon it, for she is placed in a very compromising situation, so that only a perpetual emphasis of her fundamental virtue could make her acceptable as a tragic heroine to a public with a very strict view of sexual morality. He certainly achieved his end for the audiences of his time, but at a heavy cost. He engaged their sympathies at the price of Sara's credibility as a character; as she appears in the play, her original slip is

quite unexplained and at variance with her character.
This exaggeration of Sara's sexual virtue was a concession
to the taste of the time and its prejudices. Now that
these have passed away, the one-sided portrayal of her
character can only alienate the modern reader. Sara
suffers from a further defect which is characteristic of
Lessing and which arises from his inability to create
really living persons. She is too intellectually constructed. As with all Lessing's characters one feels that
she has always thought carefully of what she intends to
say before she opens her mouth. Her long speeches
follow a logical order. Even the few exclamations she
makes are marred by similes which could only be the
product of reflection ; one of the worst instances of this
occurs in the final scene, when the dying Sara exclaims as
she catches sight of her father : " Is it a quickening appari-
tion sent from Heaven, like the angel which came to
strengthen the strong ? "[1] Yet in spite of lapses such as
this Sara does at the end rise to some measure of strength
through her calm resignation and composure in the hour
of death.

The character of Mellefont also presented Lessing with
a very grave problem which he was only able to solve in
part. As the choice of the excellent Sara he must be
made more than a mere plausible and attractive seducer.
He must have more worthy qualities, a goodness of heart
and an innate moral sense, if Sara's moral perception is
not to be at fault. And yet at the same time he *is* a
seducer, for all the responsibility for Sara's lapse must fall
on him. And thirdly, he is weak, vacillating and vain,
and it is these qualities which cause his own and Sara's
destruction. His wavering inconstancy is most manifest
in the second act,[2] whilst his weak fear of a permanent
union appears in the fourth[3] where it even draws a

---

[1] " Oder ist es eine erquickende Erscheinung vom Himmel gesandt, gleich
jenem Engel, der den Starken zu stärken kam ? " (PO. 1, 296.)

[2] Scenes iv, vi and vii.

[3] Scenes ii and iii.

rebuke from his servant, Norton. Marwood's chance of poisoning Sara is the result of his conceited wish to hear his own admiration of Sara's looks confirmed from the mouth of his former mistress. Lastly, he is never honest and straightforward with Sara, conceals the fact that he has a child by Marwood, lies to her about his reasons for postponing the wedding and even presents Marwood under an assumed name, so that at the moment he is in league with his old love against the new, yet all the time without the slightest awareness that he is being most unfair to Sara. To redeem such a despicable character convincingly was beyond Lessing's power. Mellefont shows up favourably only in his remorse after Sara's illness and death, and there are after all few who would not feel remorse in such circumstances. For the rest, Lessing depends on the statements and attitudes of the other persons to Mellefont. We have therefore to take the favourable aspects of his character on trust from the remarks of Sara and Sir William, a most unsatisfactory device. Lessing has in fact only succeeded in portraying Mellefont as the weak evil-doer, leaving Sara's affection for him and her fall almost unexplained.

The most successful of the principal characters is Marwood. She is stronger and more resolute and so a more interesting personality than the more passive Sara. Ten years later Lessing himself conceded that the virtuous character had serious disadvantages in literature, since it tended to be passive and to be overshadowed by the more active imperfect character[1] and this is in fact what occurred in *Miss Sara Sampson*. Marwood, though angry and jealous, is a most calculating woman, fully conscious of her aims and, as long as she remains calm, an ideal figure for Lessing's logical presentation of character. He fails with her, too, when passion should get the better of intelligence[2] and in her most unreal monologues.[3] He

---

[1] *Materialien zum Laokoon*, 3, lx. (PO. 4, 443.   MK. 4, 234.)

[2] Act II, sc. vii.   (PO. 1, 250.)

[3] Act IV, sc. vi, viii and ix.   (PO. 1, 277 ff.)

I

is at his best with Marwood in the scene where she reveals her true identity to the terrified Sara.[1]

The remaining characters cannot be said to be anything more than types. Sir William is the kind, considerate, sentimental father; Waitwell, the faithful servant. Neither is really individualized. Betty and Norton, the servants of Sara and Mellefont respectively, do not exist in their own right, but fulfil the functions of the confidant in French tragedy, enabling the principals to talk of their state of mind without having recourse to the unnatural soliloquy. In Norton, however, there is a trace of life, first in his compassion for Sara[2] and secondly in his affirmation of the common people's unspoiled and genuine reaction to emotion :

Mellefont : Only the lower classes are at once beside themselves if fortune should smile on them.

Norton : Perhaps because the lower classes are still capable of genuine feeling, which in the well-to-do is corrupted and enfeebled by a thousand unnatural ideas.[3]

I have made much of the faults of this play, which are indeed such as to render the work unplayable to-day and very nearly unreadable, and yet there is something to be said on the credit side, even from a strictly artistic standpoint. There are several effective scenes, notably the second interview of Sara with Marwood[4] and Mellefont's wavering at his first interview with Marwood, followed by his resolute return.[5] Psychologically this is also the most convincing part of the play. The moment he leaves Marwood and has time for reflection, his better self reasserts itself and he returns to her full of an anger which, though actually directed at her, is subconsciously concerned with his own weakness.

Miss Sara Sampson has, apart from all aesthetic con-

[1] Act iv, v, vi, vii and viii. (P.O. 1, 77, ff.)   [2] Act I, sc. vii, Act IV, sc. iii.

[3] *Mellefont :* Nur der Pöbel wird gleich ausser sich gebracht, wenn ihn das Glück einmal anlächelt.
Norton : Vielleicht, weil der Pöbel noch sein Gefühl hat, das bei Vornehmern durch tausend unnatürliche Vorstellungen verderbt und geschwächt wird. (PO. 1, 273.)

[4] Act IV, sc. viii.   [5] Act II, sc. iv, v, vi.

siderations, a very profound historical significance. The eighteenth century had been an age of imitation of French drama in Germany up to this point.   Lessing, not content with polemical writings against the French influence in the theatre and in favour of the English drama, now took the decisive step of actually writing and publishing a play in the English manner.   *Miss Sara Sampson* is therefore an essay in practical criticism of the first importance.   And not only does its success mark a vital phase in the replacement of French taste by English, more congenial to the German cast of mind ;   it is also a step toward the reaffirmation of the rights of the heart, of the emotional aspect of man, so grievously neglected by the prosaic rationalism of the first half of the century. And lastly, in opening the stage to a realistic presentation of contemporary men and women, it laid the foundation for what has ever since been one of the principal forms of tragedy; for the drama of the Naturalists of the late nineteenth and early twentieth century is a development of the "domestic tragedy" which Lessing first acclimatized on the German stage with *Miss Sara Sampson.*

2. LESSING'S FAUST

From the comfortable middle-class environment of *Miss Sara Sampson* to the magic and devilry of the Faust legend seems a far cry, and yet Lessing's interest in both of these is to be attributed to the same influence— his newly-won admiration for the English dramatists. While *Miss Sara Sampson* is derived from the sentimental novel and domestic tragedy of the eighteenth century, Faust is the result of his interest in the Elizabethans. The connection is made obvious from the context of the only fragment of his *Faust* which Lessing ever published. This scene was appended to the famous seventeenth *Literaturbrief* in which Lessing appeared decisively as the champion of Shakespeare.

All that now remains of Lessing's *Faust* is the following :

(1) A scenarium of a prologue and four scenes of the first act; in the prologue a company of devils appears at midnight before Beelzebub in a ruined cathedral; they narrate their actions. Faust is mentioned and one of the devils undertakes to seduce him from his allegiance to God. In the first scene of the first act Faust sits over his magic books and utters a spell. In response a devil appears in the second scene who pretends to be the spirit of Aristotle. Faust then proceeds in the third scene to summon a demon. In the fourth this demon appears. The greater part of this fragment is in the form of a prose sketch. Only a part of the second scene and two lines of the fourth are in dialogue.

(2) The scene printed in the seventeenth *Literaturbrief*, where Faust summons seven devils and chooses the swiftest. His choice falls upon the one who is as swift as the transition from good to evil. This scene is fully worked out in dialogue. It is the third scene of the second act.

The first reference of Lessing to his *Faust* occurs in a letter dated 12th December, 1755, but Mendelssohn had already alluded to it in a letter of the 19th November, 1755. He was still at work on it in 1758. The publication of the fragment bore the date 16th February, 1759. There followed an interval of several years. He then wrote to his brother from Hamburg on 21st September, 1767 : " I intend to have my *Dr Faust* performed here this winter. At any rate I am working at it with all my strength."[1] A suspicion that the gap between these periods of interest may correspond to two distinct versions is confirmed by a letter of von Gebler to Nicolai (9th December, 1775)—" My friend confided to me personally that he had treated the subject twice, once on the lines of the familiar fable and then without any

---

[1] " Ich bin willens, meinen Dr. Faust noch diesen Winter hier spielen zu lassen. Wenigstens arbeite ich aus allen Kräften daran."

devilry, when an arch-villain takes over the part of the black seducer against an innocent man. Both versions only need the final touches."[1] Lessing apparently destroyed his manuscript,[2] but from these indications and from accounts left after his death by two of his friends[3] it is possible to form some idea of the nature of the original versions.

The first version, to which the published fragment belonged, lay nearer to the popular legend and was the bolder in execution. The influence of the English dramatists encouraged him to portray the fantastic world which he found in the old books. The end can only be inferred. It seems unlikely that Lessing would consent to the damnation of such a seeker after knowledge as Faust, but no evidence is available. Our information over the later version is fuller. Here Faust is apparently carried off by the devils; it then appears that the whole action was a dream. Faust awakes and thanks providence for the warning.

This second version to which the scenarium apparently refers is evidently affected by the conditions and prejudices of Lessing's own time. The magic is only admissible for him in the form of a dream. Moreover, the tragic ending of man's struggle for knowledge was unacceptable to an age which believed so firmly in moral progress. Nevertheless Lessing's determination to tackle this fantastic subject indicates his superiority to the average rationalistic mind of his age. He had hit upon and sought to give form to a subject profoundly significant to the German imagination. The limitations of his age prevented him from bringing the work to a satisfactory conclusion, yet that he should have attempted

[1] " Mir hat unser . . . Freund . . . mündlich anvertraut, dass er das Sujet zweimal bearbeitet habe, einmal nach der gemeinen Fabel, dann wiederum ohne alle Teufelei, wo ein Erzbösewicht gegen einen Unschuldigen die Rolle des schwarzen Verführers vertritt. Beide Ausarbeitungen erwarten nur die letzte Hand."

[2] It is thought probable by some writers (e.g., Petsch) that the MS. was in a trunk which was lost in 1775.

[3] Hauptmann von Blankenburg and J. J. Engels.

it at all proves how much wider Lessing is than the movements of his time.

3. PHILOTAS

The experiment with *Faust* coincides in time with another quite different dramatic experiment.   In spite of the success of *Miss Sara Sampson*, Lessing had no intention of devoting himself to writing for the theatre as his principal field of activity.   His work during the next few years was largely critical and his researches into the drama of the Greeks and Romans, begun with the work on Plautus in the *Beyträge*, were pushed a stage further and his attention began to concentrate itself upon Sophocles. This interest expressed itself in the usual way with Lessing—critical works (e.g., 17 *Literaturbrief*, *Life of Sophocles*) and in addition a practical attempt to open this new field for the German stage.   The play resulting from this effort, *Philotas*, was preceded by a fragment not without interest, on a very similar theme, entitled *Kleonnis*. If the treatment and setting of these plays have their origin in Lessing's Greek studies, their spirit arises from current events.   The Seven Years' War was now in progress and Lessing, though Saxon-born, was a Prussian patriot. But Lessing's ardour is always tempered with reason and in *Philotas* he abstains from any reference to current events and simply presents the patriotic character in its highest form.

The theme of both the plays is identical.   A prince goes forth for his first campaign, at a moment when his father, incapacitated by wounds, cannot accompany him.   He is made prisoner (the *Kleonnis* fragment ceases just before this point, but it is obvious that it would have followed the same course as *Philotas*), discovers that the son of the king, whose prisoner he is, has likewise been captured, and thereupon kills himself, so that his own father may be able to exact a full ransom for his prisoner and thereby end the war successfully.   In *Kleonnis* the action is viewed from the position of the father, awaiting news of his son. Lessing doubtless realized that this would allow insufficient action and would give no opportunity of portraying the struggle in his son. Accordingly in *Philotas* he begins the action after the prince (Philotas himself) has been captured and sets the play in the camp of his captor.

As might be expected, the emotions and sentiments actuating the characters are martial ones. Patriotism, honour and love of glory dominate the mind of Philotas, together with shame at the stain which captivity brings to his honour. Of all these sentiments, the patriotism is intended by Lessing to be the predominating one. Nevertheless there is another factor which deprives the patriotic motive of some of its force, and this is the filial piety of Philotas. As his father is the only representative of the state in the play, Philotas' sacrifice may be regarded as an act of filial devotion rather than of patriotism. Lessing does his best to counter this difficulty by making Philotas stress above all the political prestige and glory of his father. Philotas is ruthless in his devotion to father and hence to fatherland, as may be seen in the ruse by which he obtains from his captors the sword with which he intends to kill himself. Lessing, by his approval of the character of Philotas, gives his support to the view that any breach of faith is justified if it furthers the interests of one's country, a belief which has characterized every German statesman from Frederick the Great to the present day. That it should occur in so just and reasonable a person as Lessing indicates how deeply this extreme patriotism is rooted in the German mind.

Although he makes no attempt to imitate the formal details of Greek tragedy, Lessing has sought to reproduce its general effect. Plot and development are extremely simple. The action begins within an hour of its final catastrophe. The details of the previous events are gradually revealed both to the persons of the play and to the spectators somewhat after the manner in which the revelation takes place in *Oedipus*. There are only four characters and the action is continuous, without division of acts. No concession is made to the demand for a "love-interest," created by French taste and then current in Germany. No woman in fact appears. In this attempt at a Greek play, Lessing had come very near creating a new form for contemporary drama. If he could have taken the further step of combining the modern setting and characters of *Miss Sara Sampson* with the simplicity and progressive exposition of *Philotas*, he would have come very near to creating the dramatic form of Ibsen a hundred years before its actual appearance.

The weakness of the play, as so often with Lessing, is its dramatic speech, which is here subjected to an exceptionally severe test by the numerous long monologues. Short speeches, first by one character then another, do something to conceal the ratiocination which pervades Lessing's dialogue and prevents it from coming to life, and the presence of several characters obliges the author to pay some heed to the characterization of their speech, so that they may be adequately differentiated. But in *Philotas* these factors were not involved and consequently the speech is similar in tone for all the characters and is far too logically constructed, as will appear from this sample of Philotas' deliberations on the problem of his suicide :

But I ? I, the seed, the bud of a man, do I know how to die? It is not only man in his maturity, who must know how to die. The youth too, and the boy must know how to, or if not, he knows nothing. He who has lived ten years, has had ten years in which to learn how to die, and what one cannot learn in ten years, cannot be learned in twenty, thirty or more.[1]

The real reason for such defective dialogue in Lessing is that, not being a creative writer, he lacks the gift of

[1] " Aber ich ? Ich, der Keim, die Knospe eines Menschen, weiss ich zu sterben ? Nicht der Mensch, der vollendete Mensch allein muss es wissen ; auch der Jüngling, auch der Knabe ; oder er weiss gar nichts. Wer zehn Jahre gelebt hat, hat zehn Jahr Zeit gehabt, sterben zu lernen ; und was man in zehn Jahren nicht lernt, das lernt man auch in zwanzig, in dreissig und mehrern nicht." (PO. 1, 316.)

getting into the skin of his characters; they are not a part of himself, they are ideas of his ; thus *Philotas* is simply the product of a very noble idea of Lessing.   And though Lessing's characters speak and act plausibly they do not convince us that they are living, because Lessing has not *felt* himself the emotions of which they speak, he only lets them say what he *thinks* such a character would say in such circumstances.   Though *Philotas* was written in prose it is of interest to note that the earlier fragment, *Kleonnis*, was in blank verse ; this was Lessing's first experiment with this metre.

CHAPTER IX

THE MASTERPIECES

1. MINNA VON BARNHELM, 1767

Philotas was not the only work of Lessing which owed its inception to the war. A far more famous and popular work, the comedy *Minna von Barnhelm*, derived its setting and its principal male character from the effect of the war and its cessation on Lessing's mind. Although Lessing himself set the date 1763 on the title-page as the date of completion, this is inaccurate, probably deliberately so, for the work was drafted in 1764 and not completed until the winter of 1766–7. By antedating the work, Lessing was seeking to emphasize its close connection with the war, which had at last reached its conclusion in that same year 1763.

The connection of the play with such repercussions of the war as were familiar to the civilians at home will become evident from a brief account of the plot. The action takes place in an inn immediately after the conclusion of hostilities (though the name is not mentioned it is evident that this inn is situated in Berlin). Major von Tellheim has been retired from the army at the end of the Seven Years' War, under suspicion of misappropriation of funds. Smarting under this disgrace to his honour (he is actually entirely innocent), he ceases to communicate with his affianced bride, Minna von Barnhelm, who lives in Saxony. The lady, who dearly loves him, undertakes the journey to Berlin in company with her maid in order to seek him out. By chance she alights at the very inn from which, incensed at the cavalier treatment meted out to him in his straitened circumstances by the inn-keeper, he is about to retire. A recognition takes place, but Tellheim obstinately insists on renouncing the hand of Minna in consequence of his changed fortunes. Nothing will induce him to alter his intentions until Minna pretends that she is disinherited and in distress. At once he is all affection and chivalrous protection, but now Minna, intent on punishing him, will have none of him. Suddenly Tellheim's fortunes are altered by a letter from the King (Frederick the Great, of course, though he is not named) absolving him from all the charges and reinstating him in the army. Minna's plan to punish him by means of a ring which she pretends to return to him (actually it is his own which by a most complex intrigue has fallen into her hands) very nearly leads to disaster, which is fortunately retrieved by the appearance of Minna's uncle to give his blessing and end the play happily.

Such characters as Tellheim,[1] and the retired serjeant-major (Werner) must have been familiar to the audiences of Lessing's day. As Lessing treated them they were bound to appeal to a public newly awakened to the virtues of patriotism. This patriotism finds direct expression in the interview between Tellheim and Werner, where the former reads the serjeant-major a lecture on good and bad soldiering :

One must be a soldier for one's country, or out of love for the cause for which one fights. To serve here to-day and there to-morrow, without any set purpose, is to go about like a butcher's man, no more.[2]

The same spirit is manifested in the praise of the Prussian King as symbol of the fatherland.[3] There is something deeper, however, than this patriotism immediately engendered during the war. These years have strengthened in Lessing a conviction which was already ripening in him before the war began, a conviction and a consciousness of his *German* nationality. One must recall that " Germany " was at that time a geographical

[1] Lessing undoubtedly had in mind his friend Kleist, who was killed in 1759, when delineating Tellheim. See above, p. 15.

[2] "Man muss Soldat sein für sein Land, oder aus Liebe zu der Sache, für die gefochten wird. Ohne Absicht heute hier, morgen da dienen, heisst wie ein Fleischerknecht reisen, weiter nichts." (PO. 2, 53. MK. 2, 96.)

[3] Act V, sc. ix.

expression without any political significance, for outside the two great states of Austria and Prussia the territory occupied by the German-speaking peoples was divided into innumerable petty states. Lessing, though a Saxon, identified himself with the energetic Prussian state, from which the unity of Germany was eventually to proceed, and showed in this his customary vision. *Minna von Barnhelm* is the expression of this new awareness of German nationalism. All the characters but one are German, and all except the inn-keeper are fundamentally honest and kind-hearted. Opposed to them is the single foreign character, the deceitful, morally decadent Frenchman Riccaut. For the first time national solidarity appears in topical form in German literature.

The national element in *Minna von Barnhelm* largely accounts for its astonishing popularity, but all this in no way determines its artistic merit. The comedy is constructed round a skeleton of intrigue, but this intrigue accounts for very little of the comic effect, which is either directly comedy of character, or else comedy of situation depending ultimately on character. The pure comedy of character occurs chiefly with the minor rôles. Tellheim's servant, Just, gruff and honest with a partiality for home-truths; Werner quick to anger but equally quick to forgive and consumed with martial ardour; the inn-keeper with his combination of cupidity, inquisitiveness and naïve fair-speaking; and Franziska, whose kindness of heart is well seasoned with vivacity and impudence, are all comic in greater or less degree in themselves. Nor should Riccaut be forgotten, whose social pretensions and begging intentions contrast with amusing effect. The comedy of situation on the other hand appears with the two principal characters. When Minna deceives Tellheim so benevolently with the ring and later when she simulates poverty, there are truly comic situations, but there are two other aspects which, though intended to be amusing, can only be accepted as such with reserve. These are Tellheim's refusal to marry Minna on chivalrous grounds and his disgust with what he assumes to be an attempt on her part to break with him. The former produces of course the stock comic situation of the woman courting the man, whilst the latter is amusing up to a point as a misunderstanding between lovers, but both are misunderstandings which border on the serious ; and as they are derived from the serious and laudable side of Tellheim's nature, so the spectator's amusement is qualified with pity and concern. And this touches a very important point : *Minna von Barnhelm* is at least as serious and sentimental as it is comic.

It is quite evident that it was Lessing's intention to touch the emotions more than to amuse. That the one aim sometimes nullifies the other is a fault in his execution. The bias on the serious side is already given by Tellheim, who is unquestionably a serious character. Lessing is at great pains to stress on all occasions the admirable and worthy aspects of his nature. Though choleric, he is just and even affectionate with his servant.[1] His generosity leads him to renounce a sum of money owing to him, as he can thereby assist the widow of the debtor,[2] and the same generosity proves to have been the cause of the accusations falsely directed against him.[3] His sane words on war and patriotism[4] prove that his undoubted valour is in the control of his reason. All these are qualities which merit admiration and in no way deserve to be exhibited in a comic light. It is true that his ideas of honour may appear exaggerated (though they would certainly appear less so in Lessing's day than now), yet this is a small fault when set against his numerous solid qualities. Tellheim already seems a somewhat unsuitable character for a comic hero, but in addition to all this he lacks one quality, which, when considered with his virtues, finally disqualifies him—there is not so much as a grain of humour in his make-up. The result is that

[1] Act I, sc. iv and viii. [2] Act I, sc. vi.
[3] Act IV, sc. vi. (PO. 2, 69–70. MK. 2, 117–8.)
[4] See above p. 131.

such a character appears ill-treated when set in comic situations. Minna to be sure, with her playfulness and love of teasing, appears more comic. Yet the kindness of heart which might redeem the scenes of misunderstanding is less manifest then than at various moments when Tellheim is not present, such as her first dialogue with Franziska,[1] her good-will towards disabled soldiers,[2] and her misplaced generosity towards Riccaut.[3] Opposite her serious lover her teasing seems cruel, like a cat playing with a mouse. She goes to the length of continuing her tormenting for mere sport, her object being already achieved.[4] In so doing she very nearly defeats her own ends, for at one moment Tellheim turns upon her with the bitterest indignation. This reaction is only natural, given Tellheim's character, but it is questionable whether the rapid reconciliation, which ensues on the appearance of Minna's uncle, is consistent with Tellheim's nature. It is indeed doubtful whether a man of his integrity and truthfulness would so readily have forgiven her deceit.

As with all Lessing's dramatic works the characters are completely open. They mean what they say and no hidden motives complicate their interplay. Yet though Lessing's emotions may not be profound, they are here entirely implicated in the characters of the play and in its national bearing, and this has resulted in a work of more than usual life. In consequence of the vividness of its characterization and of the genial good-humour which is its prevailing mood, *Minna von Barnhelm* has remained one of Lessing's most popular works. As a comedy it may have its defects, as a document it is convincing proof of Lessing's generous humanity.

2. EMILIA GALOTTI, 1772

The history of this tragedy is a curious one, in which the development of Lessing's views on the theatre may be

---

[1] Act II, sc. i.　　　　　　　　[2] Act II, sc. iii.
[3] Act IV, sc. ii.　　　　　　　　[4] Act V, sc. ix.

followed in its principal phases. In 1754 Lessing had
published in the third number of his *Theatrical Library* a
very full account of a tragedy entitled *Virginia* by
Augustino de Montiano y Luyando, a contemporary
Spaniard. This play, mentioned with evident approval
by Lessing, is on French classical lines—the three unities
are observed, the principal characters are accompanied
by confidants, the action takes place off-stage and the
speeches are inordinately long. This is the first stage,
representing Lessing's interest concentrated on the story
of Virginia in dramatic form according to French taste.
The next phase is seen in the fragment called *Virginia,*
which consists of the opening scene of a Virginia tragedy
in prose. This was long thought to be an original work
of Lessing, but has since been proved to be a translation
of the blank-verse *Virginia* of the English author, H. S.
Crisp. Lessing's interest is still in the legend in its
classical setting, but has been transferred to a play in the
English taste. Now followed the first original work of
Lessing on this theme. In a letter to Nicolai of 21st
January, 1758, he writes, referring to himself in the
third person, " His present subject is a middle-class
Virginia, to which he has given the title *Emilia Galotti.*
He has in fact separated the story of the Roman Virginia
from all the elements which made it of interest to the
whole state ; he thought that the fate of a daughter, who
is slain by her father and who esteems her virtue above
her life, is tragic enough in itself and will suffice to move
the whole soul, even though no political revolution
ensues."[1] This version consisting of only three acts has
been lost, but from various indications it is clear that it
corresponded roughly to the present form of the tragedy,
though more loosely constructed (" he avails himself

[1] " Sein jetziges Süjet ist eine bürgerliche Virginia, der er den Namen ' Emilia
Galotti ' gegeben. Er hat nämlich die Geschichte der römischen Virginia von
allem Dem abgesondert, was sie für den ganzen Staat interessant machte ; er hat
geglaubt, dass das Schicksal einer Tochter, die von ihrem Vater umgebracht
wird, dem ihre Tugend werter ist als ihr Leben, für sich schon tragisch genug
und fähig genug sei, die ganze Seele zu erschüttern, wenn auch gleich kein,
Umsturz der ganzen Staatsverfassung darauffolgte."

without hesitation of all the liberties of the English stage,"[1] wrote Lessing in the letter quoted above). In any case the decisive step was taken in this play of transferring the scene from ancient Rome to Lessing's own day. The rehandling of the play, which left it in the state in which we now know it, did not occur until Lessing was attached to the theatre in Hamburg and even then it was not completed. The final working out took place in 1772 and the work was issued in a collected edition of his plays in that year. The history of *Emilia Galotti* is therefore symbolical of the change in his orientation from French taste to English.

Lessing had introduced " domestic tragedy " into Germany with *Miss Sara Sampson*, but that play had been something in the nature of a foreign product, reeking as it did of a sentimentality quite alien to Lessing's nature. In *Emilia Galotti* Lessing succeeded in constructing a work which bore unmistakably the stamp of his own personality and which owed nothing more to English influence than the first impulsion to write " domestic tragedy." The background of the play is a petty Italian court. Its theme, as indicated above, is a modernization of the classical story of Virginia. A very beautiful middle-class girl is betrothed to a Count Appiani. The ruling Prince sees her, is enraptured by her loveliness and determines to possess her. The news of her immediately impending marriage dismays him momentarily, but in Marinelli he has a friend and counsellor at hand who undertakes to arrange the matter to the Prince's satisfaction. After a vain attempt to persuade Appiani to travel on business of state, Marinelli has recourse to violence. He causes the carriage, in which the betrothed couple are journeying to their wedding, to be attacked ostensibly by brigands outside the Prince's summer residence. Appiani is killed and Emilia brought into what she believes to be safety in the palace. There Emilia's father learns from the Countess Orsina, a discarded mistress of

[1] " Er braucht ohne Bedenken alle Freiheiten der englischen Bühne."

the Prince, the fate that will assuredly befall Emilia. When he communicates this news to the latter, she persuades him to stab her. The curtain falls as the horrified Prince dismisses his evil counsellor Marinelli.

The construction of *Emilia Galotti* is exceptionally clear and careful. There are two decisive points of action, the assault in which Appiani is killed and the death of Emilia. These occur in the third and fifth acts respectively. The intervening acts and scenes are used with great skill to prepare for these striking events. The first act is devoted entirely to the Prince and Marinelli. All the facets of the Prince's character are exposed in turn. The opening monologue shows his weariness and boredom ("Nothing but complaints, nothing but petitions")[1] and at the same time his unscrupulous partiality, which allows his passions to interfere in affairs of state, as he grants the petition of a certain Emilia Bruneschi simply because she is called *Emilia*. The same frivolous approach to matters of the greatest importance is deliberately emphasized in the final scene of this act, when, not content with reaffirming his approval of Emilia Bruneschi's petition (which is nevertheless, as he himself says, "No trifle")[2] he offers to sign a sentence of death "with the greatest of pleasure."[3] This unscrupulousness is the product of his leisure, boredom and absolute power. Every passion can carry him at once into evil-doing. So it is in the scene with Marinelli, when his unthinking rashness gives Marinelli as it were a blank cheque:

Marinelli : Will you give me a free hand, Prince ? Will you give your approval to anything I may do ?
Prince : Anything, Marinelli, anything that can ward off this misfortune.[4]

An insight is given into the Prince's character, however,

---

[1] Act I, sc. i.   [2] Act I, sc. viii.   [3] Act I, sc. viii.

[4] *Marinelli :* Wollen Sie mir freie Hand lassen, Prinz ? Wollen Sie alles genehmigen, was ich tue ?
Prinz : Alles, Marinelli, alles, was diesen Streich abwenden kann. (Act I, sc. vi.)

K

in other aspects than his capacity as a ruler. So capricious are his affections that his last mistress is already forgotten and the painter Conti meets with a cool reception when he brings this lady's portrait :

Prince : I scarcely remember.
Conti : Countess Orsina.
Prince : To be sure ! That commission, however, is a little ancient.[1]

In the same interview with the painter, the Prince's cultural pretentions, so common in an eighteenth-century ruler, are exposed for what they really are—a mere veneer.[2]　And finally his heedless impetuosity appears in his irresistible desire to see Emilia at once, although he has placed the entire management of the intrigue in the hands of Marinelli.[3]　One side of the picture is now filled in and the spectator's curiosity to see the object of his passion is aroused.

In the second act this desire is gratified. As the first act was given up to the characterization of the Prince and his environment, so the second is concerned with Emilia and her family.　The keynote in Emilia's character is an innate sensuality, held in check by genuine piety.　Her religious preoccupation is at once apparent.　When her father arrives from the country on her wedding morning, she is not occupied, as he imagines, with her robe, but has gone to hear mass.　Appiani too stresses this side of her nature—" I shall have a pious wife in you, Emilia."[4] Yet it soon becomes evident that her nature is more complex and passionate.　She arrives dismayed at the addresses of the Prince—" My devotions should have been more profound, more ardent to-day than ever before, yet never have they been less what they should

---

[1] *Prinz :* Kann mich doch kaum erinnern. . . .
　Conti : Die Gräfin Orsina.
　Prinz : Wahr !—Der Auftrag ist nur ein wenig von lange her. (Act I, sc. ii.)

[2] Act I, sc. ii.

[3] Act I, sc. vii.

[4] "Ich werde eine fromme Frau an Ihnen haben haben." (Act II, sc. vii.)

be."[1]   The three characters who surround Emilia are
also delineated.   The father, Odoardo, is revealed as
hasty and impetuous in his whirlwind visit and swift
anger with his wife.   Emilia's mother is short-sighted,
foolish and vain, whilst Appiani is worthy and serious-
minded, yet showing independence in his refusal of the
Prince's offer of employment, and courage in his
demeanour before Marinelli.   Though the principal
purpose of this act is the presentation of one set of
characters, it would have been most unsatisfactory and
dull if it had been as purely expositional as the first.
Lessing accordingly introduces into this act three distinct
incidents which advance the action.   The first of these is
the appearance of the desperado Angelo, who reveals the
plot to waylay Appiani's carriage.   The second is the
rash advance made to Emilia in church by the Prince, and
the third the appearance of Marinelli and the failure of his
first scheme to postpone the marriage and to get Appiani
out of the way without bloodshed.   The tragic conclusion is already foreshadowed by the premonitions of
Emilia and Appiani.

   The decisive event in the third act is handled with skill.
The quiet conversation of the Prince and Marinelli is
interrupted by a shot.   It is clear from Marinelli's
demeanour that he is expecting the attack on Appiani, but
the spectator is maintained in suspense as to the actual
issue till the arrival of Angelo reveals that Appiani has
been killed.   Although this scene is only the first climax,
which is intended to be subordinate to the second one in
the last act (death of Emilia), yet it is actually the highest
point of the play.   Two admirable acts of exposition have
brought the play to the point where the action is fairly
engaged.   But now the interest flags.   The exposition
consists of the analytical presentation of a given situation,
and in this critical examination as it were, of the human
relationships of the play, Lessing excelled.   But from the

---

[1] "Nie hätte meine Andacht inniger, brünstiger sein sollen als heute.   Nie ist
sie weniger gewesen, was sie sein sollte."   (Act II, sc. vi.)

murder of Appiani on, it was necessary to build up, to create ; Lessing struggles valiantly, joining piece to piece with intelligent and painstaking thoroughness, but nothing can conceal the lack of creative ability in this vital part of the play. The action does not appear to the spectator to arise naturally and inevitably out of the characters. It is very obviously pushed along by Lessing himself.

The greater part of the third act is concerned with the relationship between the Prince and Marinelli. The Prince's dependence on the latter is purely voluntary. As soon as Marinelli ceases to produce results he is to go. This division of responsibility was necessary for the thesis underlying the play, as will be seen later on. With the fourth act the Prince's apparent moral superiority to Marinelli vanishes. He is equally ready for crime and is restrained only by the fear of publicity : " One Count more or less in the world ! Does my mode of thinking suit you ? —Agreed ! I too do not fear a little crime. But, my good friend, it must be a little noiseless crime, a little useful crime."[1] This gives Marinelli his cue to assert an ascendency over the Prince in consequence of the latter's incautious approach to Emilia in church, an ascendency which contrasts oddly with the exclusive responsibility which had been placed on the Prince in the preceding act. Towards the end of the fourth act a new character appears in the Countess Orsina. Her introduction has primarily a social purpose but also serves to open Galotti's eyes to the Prince's designs on Emilia.

After two somewhat arid acts Lessing is now faced with the cardinal problem, the motivation of Emilia's death at the hands of her father. The first step is Marinelli's announcement that Emilia must be separated from her parents until the inquiry into the death of Appiani is completed. This diverts Galotti's attention

---

[1] " Ein Graf mehr in der Welt oder weniger ! Denke ich Ihnen so recht ?— Topp ! auch ich erschrecke vor einem kleinen Verbrechen nicht. Nur, guter Freund, muss es ein kleines stilles Verbrechen, ein kleines heilsames Verbrechen sein." (IV, i.)

from vengeance against the Prince to the preservation of his daughter. But this incident does not bring Lessing appreciably nearer the justification of Galotti's act. He therefore attempts the further motivation of the catastrophe by developing the possibilities of the sensual side of Emilia's nature :

I have blood in my veins, my father ; blood as warm and young as anyone. And my senses are senses. I can answer for nothing. I know the Grimaldis' house. It is the house of pleasure. One hour there, under the eye of my mother—and so many tumults arose in my soul, which the most rigid observances of religion could scarcely quell in several weeks.[1]

Yet even so the father's blow is still not justified. So finally Lessing betrays his literary approach to the play in a device which is ludicrously inappropriate. At this moment of the most intense emotional stress, when Emilia is entreating her father to give her a mortal blow, he puts a classical allusion into the mouth of his heroine, and Galotti stabs her so that he shall not have been outdone by an ancient Roman ! The dialogue at the crucial moment deserves to be quoted in full :

Emilia : Once there was a father, who, to save his daughter from shame, plunged the first weapon which came to hand into her heart and so for the second time gave her life. But such deeds were done only in olden days. No longer is there such a father !
Odoardo : There is one, my daughter, there is one ! (*He stabs her.*)[2]

This ineptitude is followed by a scene in which Odoardo's moral rectitude is preserved in spite of this appalling act by his determination to accept the full consequences of his crime and by his unflinching attitude to the Prince.

[1] " Ich habe Blut, mein Vater ; so jugendliches, so warmes Blut als eine. Auch meine Sinne sind Sinne. Ich stehe für nichts. Ich bin für nichts gut. Ich kenne das Haus der Grimaldi. Es ist das Haus der Freude. Eine Stunde da, unter den Augen meiner Mutter,—und es erhob sich so mancher Tumult in meiner Seele, den die strengsten Übungen der Religion kaum in Wochen besänftigen konnten." (V. vii.)

[2] *Emilia :* Ehedem wohl gab es einen Vater, der, seine Tochter vor der Schande zu retten, ihr den ersten den besten Stahl in das Herz senkte—ihr zum zweiten das Leben gab. Aber alle solche Taten sind von ehedem ! Solcher Väter gibt es keinen mehr !
Odoardo : Doch, meine Tochter, doch! (Indem er sie durchsticht.) (Act V, sc. vii.)

The disgrace of Marinelli brings the play to an end. This disgrace implies a contradiction of the full responsibility which was earlier laid on the Prince.

In spite of the clarity of the construction, of some effective scenes and of many happy touches, the play is far from successful and even in the painstaking psychological motivation Lessing has failed signally. The reason is clear. He has arrived at his plot by grafting a modern setting on to a classical legend. But though the story of Virginia appealed to him, it underwent no sort of transformation in his mind which would give it one inevitable shape. Such a process of creation was outside the limits of his type of mind. His approach is an external one. He modernizes the story piecemeal so that at certain points the divergence between the circumstances and manners of ancient Rome and those of his own day introduces an incongruity which no ingenuity can entirely palliate. His weakness is clearest in the scene between Emilia and Odoardo referred to above; and not only in the passage quoted, for the prelude to this climax is a long and frigid argument between the two. Dialectical speech is abundant throughout, as in all Lessing's plays. It is a sign that the characters, though carefully thought out, do not really live with their own life. For though ratiocination may be in place in the calm discussion between the Prince and the painter,[1] it is less excusable in the conversation of Appiani and Emilia ;[2] in Galotti at his most passionate it becomes totally impossible,[3] whilst the worst example of all is in the duologue preceding the catastrophe.

Apart from all aesthetic considerations, however, the play had a most important social significance. Criticism of the circumstances of Lessing's day is already implied in the theme of the play itself, in the seduction, by ruthless violence, of a middle-class girl by a prince, and is in addition explicitly pointed by such episodes as the

[1] Act II, sc. iv. [2] Act II, sc. vi.
[3] Act V, sc. iv. Act V, sc. vi.

frivolity of the Prince in dealing with state affairs.[1] The
Prince's addiction to mistresses receives particular stress.
Orsina first satirically alludes to his passion for Emilia
with, " Only now will she begin to live—a life full of
bliss, the most marvellous jolliest life of ease !—as long as
it lasts,"[2] and then goes on to denounce the Prince's
heartlessness in bitterly indignant terms—" If we all, all
the great host whom he has deserted, were changed into
Bacchantes and Furies, if we had him among us, could
tear him, rend him, could burrow in his entrails to find
the heart which he promised to each and gave to none."[3]
    Still another characteristic of the court life of the age
receives clear condemnation. This is Marinelli, the
court favourite, who holds office as long as he ministers
successfully to the Prince's lusts. The portrayal of this
character was not entirely a 'success. Lessing had to
portray a man at once more ruthless than the Prince and
yet dependent on him. The result is a pendulum swing
between the two, first one then the other appearing the
stronger. The origin of this defect lies in a social
consideration. Though Marinelli conceives and executes
the actions, yet the purpose of social criticism made it
necessary that Lessing should attribute full responsibility
to the Prince and not mere weak acquiescence. Hence
Marinelli is by turns Pandarus and Iago, and never entirely
convincing or consistent. Yet despite defects in the
execution, the social criticism and indignation which
Lessing displays in *Emilia Galotti* constitute its most
important feature. In spite of its Italian guise, it is a just
picture of the life of so many German princelings and their
court circle. In this aspect of his play Lessing was to
have a wider and profounder influence than he could have
expected. *Emilia Galotti,* frigid tragedy as it was

[1] See above, p. 137.
[2] " Sie wird nun erst anfangen zu leben. Ein Leben voll Wonne ! Das
schönste, lustigste Schlaraffenleben—so lang' es dauert." (Act IV, sc. vii.)
[3] " Wann wir einmal alle—wir, das ganze Heer der Verlassenen—wir alle in
Bacchantinnen, in Furien verwandelt, wenn wir alle ihn unter uns hätten, ihn
unter uns zerrissen, zerfleischten, sein Eingeweide durchwühlten,—um das Herz zu
finden, das der Verräter einer jeden versprach und keiner gab ! " (Act IV, sc. vii.)

(Friedrich Schlegel was later to call it " a great instance of dramatic algebra "[1]) set the example for the use of social satire in the drama of contemporary life. The influence of the play was therefore not all of the kind Lessing would have desired. He wished to write a model tragedy which would be appreciated on aesthetic grounds ; the social element was an important background yet incidental. And it is largely for this incidental social criticism that the play has since been esteemed.

3. NATHAN THE WISE, 1779

Though a few sketches for plays occur from time to time throughout Lessing's period as Librarian at Wolfenbüttel, there was only one which he felt impelled to work out in full. The theatre had lost all power to interest him and he even disliked to talk about it. It is, therefore, by no means astonishing to find that this one completed work owed its origin to events and sentiments very far removed from any relationship to the theatre. *Nathan the Wise* (*Nathan der Weise*) is in fact the product of Lessing's theological controversy of the year 1778 and belongs more properly to the history of his religious convictions, doubts and disputes, than to the remainder of his plays, all of which were written with the requirements of the theatre in mind. Its genesis and its all-important ethical content will therefore be considered later in their proper context.[2] Here it will suffice to deal with the stylistic aspects of *Nathan the Wise*.

The play is written in blank verse and is Lessing's only completed poetic drama (or " dramatic poem " as Lessing himself more justly terms it on the title-page). It cannot be claimed that it is stylistically successful. It is true that verse had the advantage of setting the whole work on a plane remote from the would-be reality of his other plays, and so was more suited than his customary

---

[1] *Uber Lessing.*   [2] See below, pp. 179 ff.

prose to his purpose in this play, which was to express his profoundest convictions and his highest wisdom. Yet his technical incapability is obvious to the most casual eye or ear. Clumsy lines abound and he is frequently driven to insert superfluous words for no other reason than to fill in the metrical pattern. In addition to actual failure in the handling of his material in this unaccustomed form, he makes frequent use of passages consisting purely of a process of reasoning. This involves an absence of colour and richness from the verse, making it an arid medium for stage performance. Yet Lessing did not seriously consider stage performance of *Nathan the Wise*, as is suggested by the sub-title " a dramatic poem," and becomes clear from a remark in a letter to his brother Karl, where he says that a performance will probably never occur (18th April, 1779). His sober verse had at any rate this advantage, that it was above all clear, and so enabled him to set forth plainly the ideas, which were for him the essential thing in this work. *Nathan the Wise* should in fact not be judged by artistic standards, but as a moral treatise in exceptionally clear and vivid form.

4. Conclusion

In assessing Lessing's importance as a dramatist, we should take care to avoid condemning him for failure to achieve something which he had no hope and no intention of achieving. No writer has ever recognized his limitations more accurately than Lessing and his own judgment on his dramatic work is a document more enlightening than any criticism from another hand:

I am neither an actor nor a creative dramatist.[1] It is true that people often do me the honour of considering me to be the latter. But only because they misjudge me. They should not draw such generous conclusions from a few dramatic attempts, which I have ventured to make. Not everyone who takes up a brush and daubs on colours is an artist. The earliest of those attempts were written

[1] This rendering of the word *Dichter* is justified by the context.

at the age when one so readily takes inclination and facility for genius. I am very well aware that what is tolerable in the more recent ones I owe simply and solely to criticism. I do not feel the quick spring in me, which reaches the surface through its own inherent force and pours forth through that force in such abundant, fresh jets : I have to force everything up by an artificial system of pressure and pipes. I should be so poor, so cold, so short-sighted, if I had not learned in some measure, modestly to borrow from others' treasures, to warm myself at others' fires and to strengthen my sight with the spectacles of art.[1]

Lessing is in fact devoid of dramatic *genius*. His plays are constructed piece by piece with infinite care and much difficulty. With all their skilful motivation they lack the one essential. Their characters do not live. The plays are plausible, but they are not real. They are a remarkable achievement considering the limitations of the author, but they are not great plays.

Nevertheless they have other merits to compensate for their artistic failure. Four of them, *Emilia Galotti*, *The Freethinker*, *The Jews* and *Nathan the Wise*, are bearers of a social content, which in the last three is still of vital importance, whilst the greater part of his dramatic output is of the utmost historical significance. Lessing contributed to the rejection of French taste in Germany not only by his critical writings, but also in a very practical way by the production of dramatic works which formed a basis for a characteristically German body of plays. The establishment of the domestic tragedy (*bürgerliches Trauerspiel*) as as much or more the result

---

[1] " Ich bin weder Schauspieler noch Dichter. Man erweiset mir zwar manchmal die Ehre, mich für den letztern zu erkennen. Aber nur weil man mich verkennt. Aus einigen dramatischen Versuchen, die ich gewagt habe, sollte man nicht so freigebig folgern. Nicht jeder, der den Pinsel in die Hand nimmt und Farben verquistet, ist ein Maler. Die ältesten von jenen Versuchen sind in den Jahren hingeschrieben, in welchen man Lust und Leichtigkeit so gern für Genie hält. Was in den neuerern Erträgliches ist, davon bin ich mir sehr bewusst, dass ich es einzig und allein der Kritik zu verdanken habe. . . . Ich fühle die lebendige Quelle nicht in mir, die durch eigne Kraft sich emporarbeitet, durch eigne Kraft in so reichen, so frischen Strahlen aufschiesst : ich muss alles durch Druckwerk und Röhren aus mir heraufpressen. Ich würde so arm, so kalt, so kurzsichtig sein, wenn ich nicht einigermassen gelernt hätte, fremde Schätze bescheiden zu borgen, an fremdem Feuer mich zu wärmen und durch die Gläser der Kunst mein Auge zu stärken." (*Hamburgische Dramaturgie*, 101–104 Stück. PO. 5, 407. MK. 5, 373.)

of the performance of *Miss Sara Sampson* as of any critical campaign. Truly German comedy began with *Minna von Barnhelm*. These works are not, therefore, to be judged solely on their merits as plays. They are models which exercised a profound influence on the subsequent history of the German drama. It is a sound paradox that much of Lessing's work for the theatre is an aspect of his criticism. It is practical criticism in the best sense.

Lessing's importance for the theatre is that of an innovator; for the modern reader he is significant for his vivid presentation in plays of a sound ethic, the validity of which is still unchallenged.

Part Four

LESSING AND RELIGION

CHAPTER X

LESSING'S CONFLICT WITH THE THEOLOGIANS

1. THE ORTHODOX FAITH

EVEN to the cultivated reader of to-day, theology seems an arid subject, divorced from the realities of modern life. It is exceptionally difficult in our time to understand an age when theological writings were both widely read and highly esteemed. Yet if all aspects of Lessing's work and personality are to be appreciated (and the effort is worth while) it is necessary to make the attempt to understand in an historical light this feature of his day.

The orthodox Lutheran faith of the eighteenth century, in which Lessing, as the son of a Lutheran pastor, was naturally bred, was a complete and self-contained system. The essential components of its world were God and Man; the link between these two, the Scriptures, was the inspired revelation of God to Man. As the Bible was divinely inspired, it was therefore literally true in its entirety. The indispensable pillar of this system was faith. As long as the faith of the individual remained intact, the system was complete and unassailable, and it continued to be valid for a considerable number of Lutheran Christians throughout the eighteenth century. For those who accepted it, theological writings based on the Bible must have an absolute validity. Here is one reason for the popularity and respect accorded to such work.

The hold of the orthodox faith still remained strong, yet there existed at the same time a considerable body of opinion which was actually hostile to the Christian faith, and the eighteenth century is better known to-day for its freethinkers than for its theologians. Not only was the orthodox faith menaced by thinkers of repute, but it became for a time fashionable to affect free-thought. Lessing himself mentions this fad in a review of 1751 : " politeness now demands that one should pretend, as long as one is in good health, to be nothing more nor less than an atheist."[1]   The current of free-thought was responsible not only for works of purely speculative philosophy, but also for a number of direct attacks on the belief of the orthodox.

These attacks could not affect the coherence of the system of orthodoxy, but they menaced its basis of faith, as the theologians clearly perceived.   The latter reacted chiefly in two ways.   A number of theologians abandoned the strict belief of their fathers and sought to enlist the methods and achievements of the philosophers in the service of religion.   Though they did not realize it, they were no less instrumental in undermining the faith on which their religion must necessarily rest than the philosophers.   Many theologians, however, preferred to adhere to literal faith in the Bible and to counter the attacks of the philosophers by quotation of the Scriptures themselves and, not infrequently, by scurrilous denunciation of their opponents.   Both parties were characterized by a growing anxiety.   They feared, only too justly, that the trend of thought of the age would deprive them of the confidence and prestige which they enjoyed among their flock.   Some buried their heads ostrich-like in the sand, whilst others reacted to criticism of religion in an exaggeratedly irritable fashion which betrayed their nervous state of mind.

Lessing's attitude to orthodoxy is a complex one. His affection for his father softened his reaction to the family religion at a time when doubts first began to germinate in his mind, and indeed it modified his approach to it throughout his life.   But it could not

---

[1] " die Artigkeit erfordert, sich für nichts Schlechters als einen Atheisten, so lange man gesund ist, halten zu lassen." (PO. 9, 207.)

silence the questionings which arose within his mind. His doubts rapidly evolved in Leipzig, once he had met the freethinker Mylius, and it is about this period that they begin to find a place in his writings.

In 1751 he published, in *The Latest from the Realm of Wit*, the fragment of a poem entitled *Religion*. This fragment was perhaps written as early as 1748, at a time when Lessing was deeply impressed by *The Messiah* of Klopstock; in any case it is not later than his first stay in Wittenberg in 1749. Only 348 lines of the first canto were published, but Lessing prefaced them with a statement that the doubts expressed at the beginning of the work would have been allayed in its continuation. That the poem was never completed suggests that Lessing was as yet unable to give any satisfactory answer to the scepticism of the first canto. Although *Religion* is chiefly a negative poem, it reveals certain positive aspects of Lessing's religious thought which are significant for his later development. Chief among these is the recognition that religion is first an affair of the heart, to which reason then gives confirmation: " May your fire, Religion, enflame my mind ! already it enflames my heart."[1] Throughout the whole poem Lessing's serious striving towards a satisfactory religious attitude and his earnest desire to surmount the doubts which beset him, cannot fail to strike the reader.

The same serious purpose and earnest striving characterize a letter written to his father on 30th May, 1749:

> Time will prove whether he is the better Christian, who has the principles of Christian doctrine in his memory, and on his lips, often without understanding them, who goes to church and observes all the practices (of religion), just because they are customary; or he who has once prudently doubted and has reached conviction by the path of investigation, or at any rate strives to reach it. The

[1] " Dein Feu'r, Religion !
Entflamme meinen Geist ; das Herz entflammst du schon." (PO. 1, 189.)

L

Christian religion is not a thing which one should accept on trust from one's parents.[1]

The twenty-year old Lessing had discarded the faith which was the essential prop of the religion of his fathers. Their system could no longer answer for him, but he remained religious at heart and continued to strive towards a solution of his problem of faith. He betrays no joy at emancipation, but he realized that his path must lead forward and not back.

2. THE CHALLENGE TO THE THEOLOGIANS

In his early reflections on Christianity, Lessing was struck by the obvious divergence between the doctrine of Christ and the mode of life of many of those who passed as Christians. He had mentioned this in the letter to his father already cited and it occurs again in a fragment found among his posthumous papers, but dating from 1750. Here he had stated that " we are angels in theory, and devils in practice."[2] Of the many precepts of the Christian religion which seemed to Lessing to be ignored in practice, the neglect of the command to love one's enemies rendered him particularly indignant, and this neglect was conspicuous in many of the theologians whose duty it was to teach such commandments. Intolerance in religious matters was anathema to him, and an intolerant attitude, whether on the part of atheist or theologian, was enough to range Lessing on the other side at once. He had indeed castigated the intolerance of the free-thinkers in his early play *The Freethinker*.[3] In

[1] " Die Zeit soll es lehren, ob der ein bessrer Christ ist, der die Grundsätze der christlichen Lehre im Gedächtnisse, und oft ohne sie zu verstehen, im Munde hat, in die Kirche geht, und alle Gebräuche mit macht, weil sie gewöhnlich sind ; oder der, der einmal *klüglich* gezweifelt hat, und durch den Weg der Untersuchung zur Überzeugung gelangt ist, oder sich wenigstens noch darzu zu gelangen bestrebet. Die Christliche Religion ist kein Werk, das man von seinen Ältern auf Treu und Glauben annehmen soll."

[2] " Der Erkenntnis nach sind wir Engel, und dem Leben nach Teufel." (PO. 20, 102. MK. 6, 304.)

[3] See above pp. 109 ff.

the fragment mentioned above, the title of which was *Thoughts on the Moravians*, Lessing turned upon the theologians. The essay is a timely plea for the toleration of this heretical Protestant sect. The essay, however, remained unfinished and unpublished and so constitutes only a pointer to the way in which Lessing's mind was moving.

Lessing's failure to present this work to the public does not in any way imply a lack of courage. Throughout his life he felt an impulse to do battle with the orthodox theologians, an impulse which Nicolai summed up in his letter to Lessing of 10th November, 1770 : " I know the itch you have long felt, to come to grips with the theologians. As if that would be very pleasant ! "[1] Lessing had in fact written throughout his life a series of works which were in some sense challenges to the theologians. The series opened as early as 1753, with the defence of Simon Lemm against the onslaughts of Luther, an essay which has already been considered in Lessing's critical work.[2] Luther had been sharply taken to task for his intolerant attitude, though Lessing was willing enough to find historical excuses for it.

In 1754, Lessing published a series of *Rehabilitations*. They were four in number, of which one, the *Rehabilitations of Horace*, was purely literary.[3] The remaining three however belonged to the theological sphere. Lessing set out to overthrow the unjust judgments passed by the theologians of his own time on three theologians of an earlier day, Hieronymus Cardanus (1501–1576), the anonymous author of the *Ineptus Religiosus* (1656) and Johann Cochläus (1479–1552). The reputations of these scholars seem now a matter of indifference, but Lessing's interest was more than that of the scholar in his search for truth, more than the hatred of injustice. It

---

[1] " Ich kenne den Kitzel, den Sie schon lange hegen mit den Theologen handgemein zu werden. Als ob das so eine Lust sein würde ! "

[2] See above, p. 45.

[3] See above, p. 74.

was once more a challenge, though an indirect one, to the theologians of his day; for he accuses them, not merely of the acceptance without investigation of a traditional view, but of deliberate falsification, above all in the essay on the *Ineptus Religiosus*.

A long interval ensued after the publication of the *Rehabilitations*, during which Lessing was preoccupied above all with critical work. The tacit renunciation of critical journalism, which coincided with his establishment in Wolfenbüttel as Librarian, once more set his energies free to pursue the theological and philosophical studies, to which he had only been able to pay spasmodic attention, chiefly while in Breslau, in the last sixteen years. Not only had he time and energy available, but the Library also held for him a vast quantity of new material. The very first year of his appointment witnessed a revival of his theological interest in a treatise entitled *Berengar of Tours* (*Berengarius Turonensis*), published in 1770.

Berengar was a cleric of the eleventh century who had been accused and condemned for heretical opinions on the doctrine of Transubstantiation. The theologians had alleged that he had eventually confessed the error of his ways and had allowed his opponent, Lanfranc (later Norman Archbishop of Canterbury) to be right on all points. Among the manuscripts of the Wolfenbüttel Library, Lessing discovered one which he proved to be a work in which Berengar, so far from admitting the justness of Lanfranc's views, actually refuted him at every point. The very existence of this work had been denied by theologians, Lutheran as well as Catholic.

Even in a purely technical aspect this work is an admirable example of Lessing's method. He first argues the probability of his case, and only when its plausibility is clear does he play his trump-card, the newly-discovered manuscript, which substantiates his case beyond all doubt. With this document in hand he discloses step by step all the intrigues of Berengar's opponents. So vividly is the work conceived that it has the same breathless interest as the gradual unravelling of the plot of a play.

Lessing declared in a letter to Nicolai, dated 16th February, 1771, that the writing of *Berengar of Tours* had given him more pleasure than that of any other of his works. The reason was deep-seated; this work, in which he once more refuted the conventional Lutheran view, enabled him to express his conviction as to the necessarily successful outcome of the pursuit of truth. Very early in the essay he makes a vigorous defence of heresy : " The thing we call a heretic has a very good side to it. It is a man who, at any rate, has tried to see with his own eyes. The only question is whether the eyes with which he has tried to see for himself were good ones."[1] The discovery that Berengar did not finally recant also encouraged Lessing in his belief in the triumph of truth. Anyone who could have persuaded Lessing that Berengar, after believing that he had found the truth, could suddenly admit himself to be wrong,

would have persuaded me, [he writes], at the same time to abstain henceforth from all investigations of truth. For what is the purpose of these fruitless investigations, if no lasting victory can be won over the prejudices of our early education ? If these prejudices can never be exterminated but at best can only be driven into flight for a longer or shorter period, then to return once more . . . No, no ! the creator plays no such cruel tricks on us ![2]

Though *Berengar of Tours* was in a sense intended to be one more provocation to the Lutheran theologians (about whom Lessing had some hard words to say in the opening pages), it produced no antagonistic reaction ;

[1] " Das Ding, was man Ketzer nennt, hat eine sehr gute Seite. Es ist ein Mensch, der mit seinen eigenen Augen *wenigstens sehen wollen.* Die Frage ist nur, ob es gute Augen gewesen, mit welchen er selbst sehen wollen." (PO. 21, 30.)

[2] " der hätte mich zugleich beredet, allen Untersuchungen der Wahrheit von nun an zu entsagen. Denn wozu diese fruchtlosen Untersuchungen, wenn sich über die Vorurteile unserer ersten Erziehung doch kein dauerhafter Sieg erhalten lässt ? Wenn diese nie auszurotten, sondern höchstens nur in eine kürzere oder längere Flucht zu bringen sind, aus welcher sie wiederum auf uns zurückstürzen. . . . Nein, nein ! einen so grausamen Spott treibt der Schöpfer mit uns nicht." (PO. 21, 45.)

rather was it conceived by the Protestant clergy as a blow directed against the Catholic party, who had always been the strongest apologists for Lanfranc in the controversy with Berengar. Somewhat to his ironical amusement, Lessing now found himself in unexpectedly good odour with the orthodox party.

Four years later, Lessing published in his *Contributions to History and Literature* an essay entitled, *Some authentic Details on Adam Neuser* (1774).[1] This essay constitutes one more rehabilitation of a character maligned by the orthodox, and one more contradiction of the views of the theologians. It is another tentative effort towards the conflict for which Lessing longed.

It was not mere combativeness which made him desire something more than a skirmish with the forces of orthodoxy. He sensed deeply the false position into which the theologians were drifting. He realized that they *dared* not investigate their own system. He felt that their loud denunciation of their opponents was intended to deafen the voice of doubt and fear within them. And he was convinced that a victory over this obscurantist attitude was inevitable, if a positive position was to be attained, which could be valid once more even for the advanced minds of the age. What that position was will appear in the next chapter.

3. THE CONFLICT

The long-desired struggle was now at last to take place. H. S. Reimarus (1694–1768), a much respected schoolmaster of Hamburg, had left in manuscript a work which had occupied him since 1743, entitled *Apologia for the reasonable Worshippers of God*. This book contained an interpretation of the Bible from an extreme rationalistic

---

[1] Neuser was a Unitarian of the sixteenth century who had settled in Constantinople where he had adopted the Moslem faith. Lessing had discovered a letter from Neuser in Wolfenbüttel, which revealed that his journey to Turkey was a flight from persecution in Europe and his conversion to Mohammedanism necessary for the preservation of his life.

standpoint. Jesus is for him a noble-minded but imprudent agitator, the resurrection an invention of the disciples, and the Christian religion based upon a deceit. Lessing obtained a copy of the manuscript from Reimarus' children and took it with him to Wolfenbüttel. It was his wish to publish it, but this enterprise was fraught with difficulties. Reimarus himself had intended the work to be reserved for a more enlightened age, and Lessing well knew that persecution would inevitably follow publication, and that the descendants of Reimarus, who were still living in Hamburg, would be more exposed to its consequences than he would be himself. The solution of this problem was the publication of fragments only and the concealment of the author's identity.

The first fragment appeared in 1774 and was of an unprovocative nature. Its subject was *The Toleration of Deists* (*Von Duldung der Deisten*), and it was received with interest and approval. In spite of its inoffensive character, Lessing proceeded with great caution. He pretended that the fragment was drawn from a manuscript in the Wolfenbüttel Library and incorporated it in the *Contributions*, together with the essay on Neuser. He led his readers along a false scent by stating that the work was anonymous, but that a certain Schmidt[1] might well have been the author. And he added a conclusion in which he deprecated the vigour of the statements of the fragment. His ruse was successful and Reimarus' reputation and his children's welfare were secured from harm.

The original fragment had still not released the storm for which Lessing hoped. But in 1777 he published five more under the title *More from the Papers of an anonymous Author, dealing with Revelation* (*Ein Mehreres aus den Papieren eines Ungenannten, die Offenbarung betreffend*). Straightway in the preface he announces that he is this time issuing something stronger, i.e., more provocative. But he is

---

[1] J. L. Schmidt (died 1749), translator of the Pentateuch (Wertheim Bible).

still circumspect. So he adds his *Antitheses* (*Gegensätze*) to the theses of Reimarus. The introductory paragraphs to these *Antitheses* contain much that is important in Lessing's struggle with the theologians. " In brief," he says, " the letter is not the spirit and the Bible is not religion. Hence objections against the letter and against the Bible are not necessarily objections against the spirit and against religion."[1] In these words he has formulated an attack upon the essential link in the orthodox system between God and Man. Lest there should be any possibility of misunderstanding his meaning, he emphasizes that " the Bible clearly contains more than is essential to religion, and it is merely hypothetical to maintain that it must be equally infallible in this superfluous matter."[2] And a thought now reappears that has already occurred in the early fragmentary poem, *Religion*, that religion depends upon *conviction* of its truth, not upon demonstrations drawn from the Scriptures or elsewhere. " Religion is not true," says Lessing, " because the evangelists and apostles taught it, but they taught it because it was true."[3] In this sentence he offered to the orthodox the weapon which would have enabled them to maintain their belief intact against the onslaught of the philosophers. To be sure it implied a sacrifice of the letter for the spirit and this was more than they were prepared to grant.

Answers to the attacks of Reimarus on the literal truth of the Scriptures soon appeared. The first in the field was J. D. Schumann of Hanover. His primary aim was to reaffirm the identity of Christianity and the synoptic gospels ; as proof, he drew first upon the fulfilment in the New Testament of prophecies contained in the Old Testament and, secondly, on the miracles recorded in

[1] " Kurz, der Buchstabe ist nicht der Geist, und die Bibel ist nicht die Religion. Folglich sind Einwürfe gegen den Buchstaben und gegen die Bibel nicht eben auch Einwürfe gegen den Geist und gegen die Religion." (PO. 22, 186.)

[2] " die Bibel enthält offenbar mehr als zur Religion Gehöriges, und es ist blosse Hypothes, dass sie in diesem Mehrern gleich unfehlbar sein müsse." (PO. 22, 187.)

[3] " Die Religion ist nicht wahr, weil die Evangelisten und Apostel sie lehrten, sondern sie lehrten sie, weil sie wahr ist." (PO. 22, 187.)

the Gospels. His tone was courteous and moderate.
Lessing's reply was contained in two brief pamphlets,
which are likewise courteous on the whole, though the
draft of a further essay, found among his papers, contains
more than a trace of irritation, the source of which is
impatience with the inadequacy of his opponent. The
first of Lessing's replies to Schumann's *On the Evidence of
Proofs for the Truth of the Christian Religion* (1777) is entitled
On Proof of the Spirit and Proof of Power (*Über den
Beweis, des Geistes und der Kraft*). Lessing pointed out that
both the proof by the fulfilment of prophecies (*Beweis des
Geistes*) and the proof by miracles (*Beweis der Kraft*)
depend upon historical truth. But historical truths are
incapable of demonstration. Hence they may not be
used to demonstrate absolute truths.[1] To the answer
that the Bible is inspired by the Holy Ghost and hence
infallible, Lessing replies, "It is unfortunately only
historically certain that these historians (the Evangelists)
were inspired and could not err."[2] This insufficiency of
historical truth as a basis for absolute truth "is the horrid
wide chasm which I cannot cross, however often and
earnestly I have tried to leap over it."[3]

Though Lessing took care to avoid identifying himself with Reimarus, he was at any rate at one with him in
regarding the evangelists as ordinary men who might err.
This view was fully worked out in an essay only published
after his death, entitled *New Hypothesis on the Evangelists,
considered as merely human Historians* (*Neue Hypothese über
die Evangelisten, als bloss menschliche Geschichtschreiber
betrachtet*). In concise paragraphs Lessing developed the
view that the four existing gospels were derived from a
single original in Hebrew. The Gospels of Matthew,
Mark and Luke are, according to him, three different

[1] PO. 23, 45 ff.

[2] "So ist das leider nur historisch gewiss, dass diese Geschichtschreiber
inspiriert waren und nicht irren konnten." (PO. 23, 49.)

[3] "ist der garstige breite Graben, über den ich nicht kommen kann, so oft
und ernstlich ich auch den Sprung versucht habe." (PO. 23, 49.)

translations of the original Gospel of the Nazarenes, as he
termed it.   The Gospel of St John is likewise based on
the original Gospel, but differs from the other three in
being an attempt to raise the new religion above the rank
of a Hebrew sect.   These views of Lessing have been
discarded by Biblical criticism, which now rejects the
theory of an original Gospel which had since been lost,
and gives the earliest place among the Synoptic Gospels
to St Mark (Lessing had considered St Matthew to be the
earliest). Lessing's essay has, however, value as the first
sympathetic attempt to investigate the evolution of the
New Testament canon in an historical light.

A new opponent soon claimed Lessing's attention.
The sixth fragment from Reimarus had contained a
summary of the discrepancies between the accounts of the
resurrection given by the four evangelists.   It was
against this fragment that J. H. Ress of Brunswick
directed his efforts.   Ress' contention was as simple as it
could well be.   The discrepancies between the various
accounts of the resurrection were, for him, purely
imaginary, a malicious invention of the author of the
fragments.

Lessing's answer to Ress was *A Rejoinder* (*Eine
Duplik*), published in 1778.   Quite early in the essay,
Lessing summarizes the basis of dispute with his
customary clarity :

My anonymous author maintains that a *further reason against*
believing the resurrection of Christ is that the accounts of the
evangelists contradict one another.

I retort : The resurrection of Christ may yet be true, *although* the
accounts of the evangelists contradict one another.

Now comes a third who says : the resurrection of Christ is to be
believed absolutely ; for the accounts of the evangelists do not
contradict one another.[1]

---

[1] " Mein Ungenannter behauptet : Die Auferstehung Christi ist auch *darum*
nicht zu glauben, weil die Nachrichten der Evangelisten sich widersprechen.

Ich erwidere : die Auferstehung Christi kann ihre gute Richtigkeit haben,
ob sich schon die Nachrichten der Evangelisten widersprechen.

Nun kömmt ein dritter und sagt : Die Auferstehung Christi ist schlechterdings zu glauben ; denn die Nachrichten der Evangelisten widersprechen sich
nicht." (PO. 23, 57.)

The thesis which Ress (who, it may be mentioned, wrote anonymously) elected to defend was an untenable one. Only sophistries and subterfuges could provide even the semblance of a case for the view that there are no contradictions between the various New Testament accounts of the resurrection. Lessing has no difficulty therefore in demonstrating the absurdity of Ress' case. His tone is at first a moderate one ; but Ress' contention that the anonymous author of the *Fragments* deliberately *refused* to see the truth presently produces a sarcastic tone in Lessing's *Rejoinder*. Its bitterness becomes vivid and entertaining when Lessing transforms his work into a monologue addressed to the supposedly sleeping Ress.[1] But the *Rejoinder* has its positive and profoundly serious side. Not only does Lessing affirm his belief that the earnest pursuit of truth is of more value than its possession, but he also claims in the most impressive terms that this work is the product of an endeavour to serve the purposes of God by " clearing slime from Thy path."[2] This passage can only be fully understood when read in conjunction with other vital utterances of Lessing, and its consideration must be deferred to the next chapter.

The struggle is now about to reach its most crucial phase. The most powerful and the most persistent of Lessing's opponents entered the lists. This was Johann Melchior Goeze (1717–1786), the Pastor of the Lutheran Church of St Catharine in Hamburg. Goeze had actually been a personal friend of Lessing while the latter was living in Hamburg. Since Lessing's removal to Wolfenbüttel, the friendship had grown cooler, to turn finally into an estrangement after Lessing had failed to reply to an inquiry made by Goeze regarding books in the Library.

In December 1777 Goeze's onslaught on Lessing as the publisher of the anonymous *Fragments* began. The campaign opened with essays in two periodicals. These

[1] PO. 23, pp. 88–9, and elsewhere.
[2] " Schlamm dir aus dem Wege räumen." (PO. 23, 117.)

newspaper articles were followed by a collection in book form, *Something provisional against the direct and indirect Attacks of Hofrat Lessing on our most holy Religion* (1778). Goeze, like Lessing himself, had a combative temperament. Unfortunately, he lacked the intelligence which rendered Lessing's aggressiveness tolerable. Goeze's method in controversy (and this was not the first in which he had been involved) was to shout and curse his opponent down. The reader should bear this in mind before passing judgment on the savage fury of Lessing's writings against Goeze.

Lessing's reply to Goeze's first attack, which was still couched in moderate terms, was *A Parable (Eine Parabel)*. The subject of this parable is the present dispute. There was once, says Lessing, a wonderful palace inhabited by a wise and benevolent king. Its architecture was peculiar and conflicted with all known rules of building. Many connoisseurs possessed plans, which they claimed to be the plans of the original builder. These plans they valued even more than the building itself. Clearly the palace represents the Christian religion, the plans are the gospels and the connoisseurs the orthodox clergy. Only a few people, Lessing continues, took another view and said : " What do your plans matter to us ? Whether it is this plan or that is all the same to us. It is enough that we learn at every moment that the most benevolent truth fills the whole palace and that from it nothing but beauty, order and well-being are spread over the whole land."[1] Such a one, who values the spirit above the letter, was Lessing himself. But now, so runs the parable, a cry of fire was heard in the building, and all that the connoisseurs would think of doing was for each to save his own plan without heeding the supposedly burning fabric. The moral is clear enough. It is a restatement of the

---

[1] " Was gehen uns eure Grundrisse an ? Dieser oder ein andrer, sie sind uns alle gleich. Genug, dass wir jeden Augenblick erfahren, dass die gütigste Wahrheit den ganzen Palast erfüllet, und dass sich aus ihm nichts als Schönheit und Ordnung und Wohlstand auf das ganze Land verbreitet." (PO. 23, 154. MK. 7, 181.)

affirmation in Lessing's *Antitheses*, that " the Bible is not religion." It is one more hint to the theologians that they are on a wrong track and are confusing superfluous details with essentials.

The *Parable* was accompanied by a *Request*. This request is moderate enough. Goeze had falsified a statement of Lessing. He had claimed that Lessing's intention in publishing the *Fragments* was to refute the Christian religion. Lessing now asks Goeze to correct this statement. Lessing's actual words had implied that the Christian religion remained intact in the hearts of the faithful, in spite of the objections which can be made against the literal truth of the Bible. As a strict Lutheran, Goeze was unable to appreciate this distinction and would in any case not have acceded to Lessing's request. Nor would he have been in any way appeased by Lessing's statement in his *Request* that Christianity is not static but in evolution, and that the sects, including of course the Lutheran, are phases which must necessarily pass : " Christianity goes its eternal gradual pace, and eclipses do not derange the planets from their courses. But the sects of Christianity are its phases, which can only endure by stagnation of all nature, when sun and planet and observer remain fixed at the same point. God preserve us from this appalling stagnation ! "[1]

Before Lessing's *Request* and *Parable* could be published, however, Goeze's tone had passed from the merely aggressive to the scurrilous. Lessing then appended to the other two essays a *Challenge* to Goeze (*Absagungsschreiben*) which culminated in the following : " Write, Herr Pastor, and let your supporters write, as much as you will ; I shall write too. If in the least point which concerns me or my anonymous author I leave your writing unanswered where you are in the wrong, it

---

[1] " Das Christentum geht seinen ewigen allmählichen Schritt, und Verfinsterungen bringen die Planeten aus ihrer Bahn nicht. Aber die Sekten des Christentums sind die Phases desselben, die sich nicht anders erhalten können als durch Stockung der ganzen Natur, wenn Sonn' und Planet und Betrachter auf dem nämlichen Punkte verharren. Gott bewahre uns vor dieser schrecklichen Stockung ! " (PO. 23, 156. MK. 7, 184.)

will mean that I am incapable of holding a pen."[1]

Before the *Challenge* was written, Lessing had prepared another assault upon Goeze. The title of this work was *Axioms* (*Axiomata*). Goeze had attacked the passage already quoted from the *Antitheses*, in which the identity of the Bible and the Christian religion had been denied. In the *Axioms*, Lessing defends this passage, sentence by sentence, from Goeze's onslaughts.

The *Challenge* had, however, inaugurated the acutest phase of the controversy. Lessing's tone in polemical writings was at all times uncompromisingly abrupt and downright. But now his pugnacity was heightened by the intolerable grief at the death of his wife and their newly-born child, a grief from which he sought to escape by a vigorous prosecution of the theological dispute. The series of pamphlets which now appeared under the title *Anti-Goeze* was not a pure product of the conflict, but was a safety-valve for Lessing's over-charged emotions as well as a counter-attack to the offensive of Goeze.

The very first *Anti-Goeze* pamphlet reveals Lessing in aggressive mood. " You can shout me down," he cries, " once a week. You know where [i.e., in the pulpit]. But you shall certainly not write me down."[2] Goeze is, according to Lessing, acting precisely counter to the spirit of Luther to whom he (Goeze) pays lip-worship :

Luther's spirit demands unconditionally that no man should be hindered in the pursuit of truth after his own fashion.[3]

The second *Anti-Goeze* brings a more violent clash between the two adversaries. Incensed at having been accused by Goeze of attacking the Christian religion,

[1] " Schreiben Sie, Herr Pastor, und lassen Sie schreiben, soviel das Zeug halten will ; ich schreibe auch. Wenn ich Ihnen in dem geringsten Dinge, was mich oder meinen Ungenannten angeht, recht lasse, wo Sie nicht recht haben : dann kann ich die Feder nicht mehr rühren." (PO. 23, 161. MK. 7, 190.)

[2] " Überschreien können Sie mich alle acht Tage : Sie wissen, wo. Überschreiben sollen Sie mich gewiss nicht." (PO. 23, 192. MK. 7, 227.)

[3] " Luthers Geist erfodert schlechterdings, dass man *keinen* Menschen in der Erkenntnis der Wahrheit nach seinem eignen Gutdünken fortzugehen hindern muss." (PO. 23, 194. MK. 7, 230.)

Lessing denounces his opponent for having fabricated a deliberate lie. It would be easy for Lessing to say that he had derived all his ideas from Goeze during their friendship. And what hinders him from inventing such a lie? "That I have not your effrontery! That alone prevents me. I do not presume to say what I cannot prove: and you—you do seven days in the week what you should do on one only; that is, drivel, slander and bluster."[1]

So the dispute goes on. Goeze's intolerance is denounced in the third pamphlet. His project that controversial writings on religion should be conducted in Latin is demolished in the fourth. In the fifth, Lessing points out that Goeze, despite his thunderous denunciations of "Popery," is heading for the re-establishment of an ecclesiastical tyranny such as that of the medieval papacy. Lessing convicts him too of deliberate misquotation of the *Fragments* and passes on him the damning verdict: "He who is capable of distorting a quotation against his better knowledge and in spite of his conscience, is capable of everything else: can bear false witness, can forge writings, can invent facts, can consider every means permissible in order to make such invented facts plausible."[2] In the eighth pamphlet, Lessing bitterly reproaches Goeze with failing to answer any of the points in the *Axioms*. "Why does he not refute my *Axioms* if he can? Why does he perpetually bring new slanders against me?"[3] Lessing himself answers this question in the eleventh *Anti-Goeze*. Goeze's aim is to incite the general public against Lessing and crude falsifications are

---

[1] "Dass ich Ihre Stirn nicht habe: das allein hindert mich. Ich unterstehe mich nicht zu sagen, was ich nicht erweisen kann: und Sie—Sie tun alle sieben Tage, was Sie nur einen Tag in der Woche tun sollten. Sie schwatzen, verleumden und poltern." (PO. 23, 201. MK. 7, 238.)

[2] "Wer fähig ist, eine Schriftstelle wider besser Wissen und Gewissen zu verdrehen, ist zu allem andern fähig: kann falsch Zeugnis ablegen, kann Schriften unterschieben, kann Tatsachen erdichten, kann zu Bestätigung derselben jedes Mittel für erlaubt halten." (PO. 23, 219. MK. 7, 259.)

[3] "Warum widerlegt er meine 'Axiomata' nicht, wenn er kann? Warum bringt er immer neue Lästerungen gegen mich auf die Bahn?" (PO. 23, 236. MK. 7, 277.)

more apt for this than the literal truth. " You shout,"
says Lessing, " that the dog is mad, well knowing what
conclusion the street-arabs will draw from this."[1]
Goeze's aim, or at any rate one of his aims, was the evic-
tion of Lessing from his office. This, as Lessing pointed
out, must necessarily follow if Goeze's allegations were
true.

The virulence with which this controversy was conducted on both sides defeated Lessing's aim in some
degree. The torrent of abuse obscured his purpose of
attaining a final settlement with the orthodox belief.
Possibly the dispute would have clarified itself and his
position would have been clearly stated in the subsequent
course of the conflict, if a drastic step had not brought the
quarrel to a sudden close.

Lessing's adversaries, led by Goeze, had not ceased to
clamour for state intervention against Lessing. On
13th July, 1778, the Duke of Brunswick instructed
Lessing that future writings on religion must be subjected
to examination by the censorship before publication.
Lessing's disappointment and anger are recorded in a very
human fragment discovered among his papers.[2] The
twelfth *Anti-Goeze* was never to be written.

There was still one controversial work which was
already in the press in Hamburg and Berlin and so
escaped the veto of the Duke. *G. E. Lessing's Necessary
Answer to a very Unnecessary Question of Herr Hauptpastor
Goeze in Hamburg* (*G. E. Lessings nötige Antwort zu einer
sehr unnötigen Frage des Herrn Hauptpastor Goeze in Hamburg* (1778) is the essay which gives some ground to the
supposition that a continuation of the controversy might
have led to positive results. For Goeze seemed at last
willing to deal with the point at issue, whether Christianity can exist independently of the Bible. He postu-
lated however that Lessing must first say what he under-

---

[1] " Sie schreien über den Hund, ' er ist toll ! ' wohl wissend, was die Jungen
auf der Gasse daraus folgern." (PO. 23, 253. MK. 7, 297.)
[2] PO. 25, 156. MK. 7, 301.

stood by " Christian religion." This is the question to which the title alludes, and with it we are once more in the realm of personal controversy. For, as Lessing pointed out, what Goeze hoped for was a damaging admission which would make Lessing's continuance in his office of Librarian impossible. Lessing accordingly returns a cautious historical answer. By " Christian religion " he understands the doctrines embodied in the symbolic writings of the Christian Church in the first four centuries A.D.

Owing to the Duke's intervention, this essay remained Lessing's last contribution to the controversy. Whether its continuation would have produced results of any value must remain a mere supposition. As it was, its one result was to shake the basis of the Lutheran faith. Lessing's effort to substitute a positive faith for the belief which he undermined failed as far as this conflict was concerned. The " itch to come to grips with the theologians " had misled him and it was only in non-controversial writings that he succeeded in offering something constructive to replace what he had demolished. This partial failure was accounted for by the fact that no adversary arose who was both able and willing to understand the points at issue. And so the much-desired conflict ended with only negative and destructive results.

CHAPTER XI

LESSING'S RELIGION

1. Speculation

WHAT Lessing did *not* believe became clear in the last
chapter. To discover what he did believe is, however,
no easy matter. There are two principal reasons for this
difficulty. In the first place his strong spirit of contradiction led him occasionally to take sides in controversies in
which his own opinions were involved on neither side.
Secondly, he was well aware that his own most sacred
convictions would not have been understood, even by
his most intimate friends, not to speak of the generality of
the readers of his day. An indication of the extent to
which he concealed his views is to be found in the fact
that, after Lessing's death, his friends Mendelssohn and
Jacobi differed radically over his philosophical opinions.
In view of this striking reticence on Lessing's part,
documents found among Lessing's papers after his death
(and never intended for publication) assume a particular
importance. They are especially helpful in throwing
light on the few published works in which his convictions
were embodied, not infrequently in somewhat cryptic
form.

Lessing's earnest striving to surmount his doubts had
already appeared in the poem *Religion*. Some four
years later he jotted down a number of precisely reasoned
paragraphs, entitled *The Christianity of Reason* (*Das
Christentum der Vernunft*). Deep down in him is the
conviction that the dogmas of Christianity must correspond to some reality, which he longs to discover. The
way of faith is barred by his doubts. The way of reason
still lies open. And so Lessing seeks, by a dialectic
process, to arrive at the meaning of the doctrine of the
Trinity. He begins by postulating the existence of
God. Here is at any rate something which he believes.

Thinking and creating (Lessing goes on to say) are one act in God. Now it is possible for God to think of Himself in two ways ; either to consider all His perfections together or to consider them singly. In the former case, God creates a being similar to Himself in all respects. This being, Lessing terms the Son of God, or preferably God the Son. The perfect harmony existing between these two similar perfect beings is the Holy Ghost, and all three are one. This dialectical process is unlikely to afford any satisfaction to anyone in our day. It is interesting because it shows that the doctrines in which Lessing had been brought up still had a strong hold upon his imagination. Even when his method is an entirely rationalistic one, the dogmas of the Christian faith are still valid for him. *The Christianity of Reason* contains another idea of significance in Lessing's later development. We have seen that God may also consider His perfections singly. The result of this activity is the creation of the world, which, according to Lessing, is a continuous process. This belief implies the oneness of God and the world ; it is pantheistic.

This hint at the nature of Lessing's views assumes much greater importance when we discover, also from unpublished papers, that he was extremely interested in Spinoza. In the draft of a letter to Mendelssohn, he compares Leibniz and Spinoza.[1] Here he lays particular emphasis on the identity of body and soul in Spinoza's philosophy and implies his preference of this identity to Leibniz' conception of body and soul as distinct. A fragment headed *On the Reality of Objects outside God* affords another confirmation. Lessing states that he can form no conception of existence separated from God. God is identical with the world. Many years later he was to write on the door of Gleim's summer-house the Greek words ἓν καὶ πᾶν, " one and all," a final cryptic affirmation of his community of thought with Spinoza.

[1] *Durch Spinoza ist Leibniz nur auf die Spur der vorbestimmten Harmonie gekommen* (PO. 24, 135. MK. 6, 339.)

As the pantheism of Spinoza was in disfavour in the
earlier part of the eighteenth century, it is evident that
Lessing is going his own way here, just as he had in his
interpretation of the dogma of the Trinity.

An essay on Leibniz (*Leibniz von den ewigen Strafen*)
published in 1773 gives a further clue.   Here Lessing (at
first sight unexpectedly) supports the view that the pains
of Hell are eternal.   His attitude is easily understood.
The torments of Hell are, in his view, a symbol for the
natural consequences of sin.   As no cause ever ceases to
have effect, so these consequences are eternal.   Once
more Lessing accepts a dogma of the Church and gives to
it his own personal interpretation.   There is an implication here, too, of belief in the continuance of existence, in
other words of the immortality of the soul.

Lessing interprets this doctrine of the Church in his
own way.   In an undated fragment headed *That it is
possible for Man to have more than five Senses* (*Dass mehr als
fünf Sinne für den Menschen sein können*) he concludes,
"This my system is certainly the oldest of all philosophical systems.   For it is really none other than the
system of the pre-existence of the soul and metempsy-
chosis."[1]   This most interesting fragment contains
another idea of the greatest importance ; that of the
progress of man, from the soul as created by God,
through the gradual acquisition of new senses, to a
definite goal, though that goal cannot be defined by
Man.[2]   Similar affirmations of progress in the discovery
of truth have already been remarked in the essay on
Berengar of Tours.[3]

So many of Lessing's beliefs have their root in
doctrines of the Church that it is worth while asking,
what was his attitude to revealed religion.   In an early
fragment *On the Genesis of revealed Religion* (*Über die Entste-*

[1] " Dieses mein System ist gewiss das älteste aller philosophischen Systeme.
Denn es ist eigentlich nichts als das System von der Seelenpräexistenz und
Metempsychose." (PO. 24, 158.)

[2] Paragraph 19. (PO. 24, 158.)   [3] See above, p. 156.

hung der geoffenbarten Religion) he makes it clear that positive religions became necessary through the variations in man, which are the result of the process of division entailed when God considers his perfections separately. " All positive religions," he maintains, " are true and false in equal degree."[1] But the full answer to this question can only be given when another problem has been solved. This is the question of freewill. Once more we reach an unexpected result. Lessing was a determinist, or, if we prefer theological terms, he was a believer in " predestination ". In his explanatory notes to the *Philosophical Essays* of W. Jerusalem,[2] Lessing has a passage in which he refers to the question of free-will in vigorous terms, which have the ring of conviction : " What do we lose if our freedom of will is denied ? Something—if it is something— which we do not need, whether for our activity here or for our happiness in the next life. Something, the possession of which must make us far more restless and anxious than the conviction of the contrary can ever make us.—Compulsion and necessity, according to which the thought of the Highest Being is effective—how much more welcome are they to me than the bare ability to act in the same circumstances, now in one way, now in another ! I thank the Creator that I am *not* free, that I must do what is *best*."[3] This determinism is expressed again in the famous conversations recorded by F. H. Jacobi[4] from the year 1780. In his remarks to Jacobi,

[1] " Alle positiven und geoffenbarten Religionen sind folglich gleich wahr und gleich falsch." (PO. 20, 194. MK. 6, 313.)

[2] This was the young man whose suicide furnished Goethe with a conclusion for *Die Leiden des jungen Werther.*

[3] " was verlieren wir, wenn man uns die Freiheit abspricht ? Etwas—wenn es etwas ist—was wir nicht brauchen, was wir weder zu unsrer Tätigkeit hier, noch zu unsrer Glückseligkeit dort brauchen. Etwas, dessen Besitz weit unruhiger und besorgter machen müsste, als das Gefühl seines Gegenteils nimmermehr machen kann. Zwang und Notwendigkeit, nach welchen die Vorstellung des Besten wirket, wie viel willkommner sind sie mir als die kahle Vermögenheit, unter den nämlichen Umständen bald so, bald anders handeln zu können ! Ich danke dem Schöpfer, dass ich *muss*, das *Beste* muss." (PO. 7, 121-2.)

[4] *Über die Lehre des Spinoza* (1785.)

Lessing openly acknowledged his adherence to the philosophy of Spinoza—" There is no other philosophy than that of Spinoza."[1] When Jacobi objected that Spinoza was a determinist, Lessing replied " I desire no free-will."[2] The deterministic attitude was not a depressing or gloomy one for Lessing ; he was perfectly sincere when he exclaimed, " I thank the Creator that I am not free." And the secret of this joy at having no free-will lies in Lessing's firm belief that God pursued a purpose with Man. This conviction of the progress of Man, of the ordering of the world by God to produce this progress, is already implicit in *The Christianity of Reason*. Such a faith makes the deterministic view tolerable and even welcome.

Lessing believed that God so arranged the world that even the errors of Man are instrumental in furthering progress. In the light of this knowledge, the deeply serious passages from *A Rejoinder* take on a new meaning. The conviction of the value even of errors explains the statement : " If God held enclosed in His right hand all truth and in His left hand the ever-living striving for truth, *although with the qualification that I must for ever err*, and said to me ' Choose,' I should humbly choose the left hand and say, ' Father, give ! Pure truth is for Thee alone ' ! "[3] And the same faith inspires what Lessing himself termed an " involuntary outburst of my most sincere sentiments "[4] later in the essay : " If I have not applied my leisure (in refuting Ress) in the best possible way, what does that matter ? Who knows whether I might have employed it still worse with something else ? It was

---

[1] " Es gibt keine andre Philosophie als die Philosophie des Spinoza." (PO. 24, 170.)

[2] " Ich begehre keinen freien Willen." (PO. 24, 172.)

[3] " Wenn Gott in seiner Rechten alle Wahrheit und in seiner linken den einzigen immer regen Trieb nach Wahrheit, obschon mit dem Zusatze, mich immer und ewig zu irren, verschlossen hielte und spräche zu mir : " Wähle ! " ich fiele ihm mit Demut in seine Linke und sagte : " Vater, gib ! die reine Wahrheit ist ja doch nur für dich allein ! " (PO. 23, 58–9.)

[4] " unwillkürlichen Ausbruche meiner innigsten Empfindung." (PO. 23, 117.)

at any rate my intention to employ it well. It was at any
rate my conviction that I could in this way employ it well.
I leave it to the passage of time to show what my honestly
stated opinion is to do and can do. Perhaps it *is not* to
have as much effect as it *might*. Perhaps, according to
the laws of a divine economy the fire is still to go on
smoking, for a long time, making healthy eyes smart,
before we can enjoy its light and heat. If that is so, then
forgive, eternal Source of all truth, which alone knows
when and where the truth is to appear, Thy vainly active
servant. He sought to clear slime from Thy path. If he
has unknowingly thrown grains of gold away with the
slime, Thy grains of gold are not lost."[1] All earnest
endeavour after truth is of value, no matter how much the
seeker may err, for God uses errors to further his ends.

It is in the light of this that Lessing's attitude to
revealed religion should be understood. The various
religions and their various phases are stages in an attempt
to reach the truth. And even though they " are false and
true in equal degree ", yet they contribute as much by
what is false as by what is true to the progress of Man.
Their dogmas are of value even though they may not be
literally true.

We are now in a position to summarize Lessing's faith.
He believed that the world and hence Man was a part of
God[2] and that the soul of man was immortal (pre-
existence and transmigration). He believed that God in
His goodness so ordered the world that Man moved

[1] " Habe ich meine Musse . . . nicht zum besten angewandt, was thut das ?
Wer weiss, ob ich sie mit etwas anderm nicht noch schlechter angewandt hätte ?
Mein Vorsatz war es wenigstens, sie gut anzuwenden. Meine Überzeugung war
es wenigstens, dass ich sie *so* gut anwenden könne. Ich überlasse es der Zeit,
was meine aufrichtig gesagte Meinung wirken soll und kann—Vielleicht *soll* sie
so viel nicht wirken, als sie wirken *könnte*. Vielleicht soll, nach Gesetzen einer
höhern Haushaltung, das Feuer noch lange so fortdampfen, mit Rauch noch
lange gesunde Augen beissen, ehe wir seines Lichts und seiner Wärme zugleich
geniessen können. Ist das, so verzeihe du, ewige Quelle aller Wahrheit, die
allein weiss, wenn und wo sie sich ergiessen soll, einem unnütz geschäftigen
Knechte ! Er wollte Schlamm dir aus dem Wege räumen. Hat er Goldkörner
unwissend mit weggeworfen, so sind deine Goldkörner unverloren." (PO. 23,
117.)

[2] In the *Christianity of Reason*, Lessing terms men " as it were limited Gods "
(*gleichsam eingeschränkte Götter*).

towards a goal determined by God. He believed that God accomplished His purpose with Man as much through error as through truth. He believed that revealed religions were phases in God's scheme and that beneath each of their dogmas lay some profound truth. And he believed that God controlled Man entirely, that is to say, that Man had no freedom of will.

Clearly Lessing's religion depends as much on faith as the orthodox belief, though the tenets which he is prepared to accept are not those of the orthodox. It is interesting to examine his view of faith. In an essay, entitled, *The Objections of Andreas Wissowatius to the Trinity*, published in 1773, he points out the peculiar meaning attached to the word " believe " by many theologians of his day. It signifies for them " to consider true for natural reasons."[1] Lessing points out that this is not " belief " at all. True belief implies that one holds something to be true which cannot be explained. Lessing recognized the incompleteness of man's knowledge and realized that faith must come to the aid of the human reason. The large part which faith plays in his religion distinguishes him from the majority of his contemporaries, and reveals the extent to which his religion is a personal one rather than that of the age.

In the year before his death, Lessing published a small book which contains confirmation of all the features of his faith as we have discovered them. *The Education of the Human Race (Die Erziehung des Menschengeschlechts)* is Lessing's testament. Here he rises above the turmoil of his age and sounds for the first time a prophetic note. " The author," he says in the preface, " has set himself on a hill, from which he believes he surveys more than the course prescribed for to-day alone."[2] This unaccustomed tone proclaims that

---

[1] " aus natürlichen Gründen für wahr halten." (PO. 21, 188.)

[2] " Der Verfasser hat sich darin auf einen Hügel gestellt, von welchem er etwas mehr als den vorgeschriebenen Weg seines heutigen Tages zu übersehen glaubt." (PO. 6, 63.)

Lessing is for once about to rend the veil behind which he had so carefully concealed his religious convictions.

The hundred brief, succinct, numbered paragraphs of *The Education of the Human Race* open with the statement that revelation is for the whole human race what education is for the individual. This identity is important for the development of Lessing's thought; for he at once alters the meaning of his terms without warning, while still preserving the relationship of education and revelation. The initial statement had taken education and revelation in the customary sense, as something coming from without, something which the individual could not acquire but for the intervention of a teacher or of God. But now Lessing affirms that "revelation gives the human race nothing which the human reason left to itself would not hit upon; it only gave and gives it these important things sooner."[1] Once this special sense of revelation is grasped, the trend of Lessing's thought becomes clear.

Revelation then is simply an accelerated knowledge. The process of the education of the human race is this: God reveals to Man truths which he is as yet incapable of grasping; in due course his reason understands these truths and the revelation then ceases to have any value. The positive revealed religions have their value for a time; they are phases, which Man outgrows.

Having established these premises, Lessing summarizes rapidly the spiritual history of Man. God first chose a single people, the Jews, as the object of education in the first phase, the " childhood " of Man. (Paras. 9, 16.) To this people he revealed the idea of a single God. In due course, the reason of the Jews brought them to an understanding of their revelation. (Para. 36.) The " schoolbook " of this revelation, the Old Testament, now became superfluous. " A better pedagogue must come and

---

[1] " Also gibt auch die Offenbarung dem Menschengeschlechte nichts, worauf die menschliche Vernunft, sich selbst überlassen, nicht auch kommen würde ; sondern sie gab und gibt ihm die wichtigsten dieser Dinge nur früher. "(Para. 4, PO. 6, 64.)

tear the school book, now exhausted, from the child's
hands : ... Christ came."[1] With Christ came a new revelation, that of the immortality of the soul. (Para. 58.)
The New Testament became the second improved
" schoolbook " of Mankind. (Para. 64.) Now Man
stands at a point where this revelation too ceases to be
necessary, as his reason has shown him the truth underlying Christ's revelation.

Having reached the present day in his swift survey,
Lessing pauses in order to deal with a subject very dear
to him, the meaning of the dogmas of Christianity.
These dogmas are rational truths revealed before Man is
capable of comprehending them with his intelligence.
We have already seen his interpretation of the Trinity.
Now he explains Original Sin, as the primitive state of
men who are incapable of following moral laws.

From interpreting the doctrines of the Church,
Lessing passes on to affirm his belief in progress, that
vital keystone to his faith :

Or is the human race never to reach these highest degrees of
enlightenment and purity ? Never ?
Never ? Let me not think such blasphemy, all-loving God :
Education has its *goal*; for the race no less than for the individual.
Whatever is educated, is educated *for* something.[2]

Man will eventually attain perfection to the point when
his conduct will be governed by the desire to act rightly,
not by arbitrary rewards. (Para. 85.) Lessing's tone becomes that of the seer, as he affirms that " the time of a
' new eternal Gospel ' will certainly come,"[3] and
supports his opinion with a reference to " certain
Mystics of the fourteenth century."

[1] " Ein bessrer Pädagog muss kommen und dem Kinde das erschöpfte Ele-
mentarbuch aus den Händen reissen—Christus kam." (Para. 53. PO. 6, 74.)

[2] " Oder soll das menschliche Geschlecht auf diese höchste Stufen der Auf-
klärung und Reinigkeit nie kommen? Nie ? Nie ?—Lass mich diese Lästerung
nicht denken, Allgütiger ! Die Erziehung hat ihr *Ziel*; bei dem Geschlechte
nicht weniger als bei dem einzeln. Was erzogen wird, wird zu etwas erzogen."
(Para. 81-2. PO. 6, 80. MK. 7, 447.)

[3] " Sie wird gewiss kommen, die Zeit eines ' neuen ewigen Evangeliums '."
(Para. 86. PO. 6, 81. MK. 7, 448.)

The book closes with a renewed confession of belief in the transmigration of souls, which Lessing held to be the truth underlying the revealed dogma of the immortality of the soul.

And so we find that almost all the tenets of Lessing's faith which it had been possible to detect in his other writings are embodied in this, his most personal work. *The Education of the Human Race* is a credo totally different from any other of Lessing's age. Through it all runs the noble thought incorporated in Para. 91 : "Go Thy imperceptible pace, eternal Providence ! But let me not lose faith in Thee because of Thy imperceptible motion.— Let me not lose faith in Thee when Thy steps seem even to go backward !—It is not true that the straight line is always the shortest."[1] In this last "unreasonable" sentence (for after all the straight line *is* the shortest between any two points), lies a clue which, coupled with other hints such as the reference to the mystics, leads us to the realization that the religion of Lessing with its peculiar blend of faith and rationalism has more affinity with the religion of mystics such as Meister Eckhart than with any acknowledged faith or philosophy of Lessing's own day.

2. LESSING'S ETHIC : NATHAN THE WISE

Most of the expressions of Lessing's faith are scattered through various works and unpublished sketches and could not at the time be pieced together. Even with *The Education of the Human Race* he deliberately obscured the issue by asserting that it was not his work. A plain hint had appeared, it is true, in 1778 with the publication of *The Testament of St John* (*Das Testament Johannis*). This pamphlet was part of Lessing's reply to Schumann

[1] "Geh deinen unmerklichen Schritt, ewige Vorsehung ! Nur lass mich deiner Unmerklichkeit wegen an dir nicht verzweifeln.—Lass mich an dir nicht verzweifeln, wenn selbst deine Schritte mir scheinen sollten zurückzugehen !—Es ist nicht wahr, dass die kürzeste Linie immer die gerade ist." (PO. 6, 81. MK. 7, 449.)

and thus belongs to the first phase of the theological controversy. Written in the form of a dialogue between Lessing and his opponent, it culminates in Lessing's declaration that St John's sole message in his old age was, "Love one another"; and that he justified its brevity thus, "because that alone suffices, adequately suffices."[1] But these few pages had been forgotten in the strife that followed, so that Lessing's contemporaries were able to form a clear idea of his views only from the play which he published in 1779, *Nathan the Wise*.

The controversy with Goeze led, as we have seen, to no positive result of any value, and might never have produced any, even if it had been continued. The intervention of the Duke, which Lessing at first so bitterly resented, was to prove a blessing in disguise. The period of depression, to which the interruption of the dispute gave rise, came to an end with a decision which Lessing communicated to his brother in a letter dated 11th August, 1778. He had formed a project of writing a play with which " I shall certainly play the theologians a worse trick than with ten more *Fragments* (of Reimarus)"[2] Lessing's first intention, as this remark would suggest, was probably a satirical comedy. But as his interest in the plan grew, his bitter resentment against his adversaries waned; already on 20th October he informed his brother that the work was not to be satirical, but " will be as moving a play as any I have ever written." *Nathan the Wise* became in fact the receptacle for all the ideas most sacred to Lessing; its removal from the sphere of controversy was a necessity if those convictions were not to be obscured by the smoke of battle.

The plot of *Nathan*, though complex, is of slight importance. It is set in Palestine at the time of the Crusades and is, in brief, a story of love between a brother and a sister, neither of whom is aware of their

---

[1] " Weil das allein . . . genug, hinlänglich genug ist." (PO. 23, 53.)

[2] " ich gewiss den Theologen einen noch ärgern Possen spielen will, als noch mit zehn Fragmenten."

blood-relationship. The revelation of this tie before any evil consequences can ensue is accompanied by the discovery that they are both the children of the deceased brother of the Mohammedan, Saladin. Yet this bare mention of the theme omits the vital central character, Nathan. From the point of view of the intrigue Nathan is indeed incidental. He serves no purpose in the plot but to bring about the discovery of the blood-relationship between the lovers. The fact that the principal figure plays a minor part in the intrigue only demonstrates that the interest of the play is independent of its plot.

What matters in *Nathan* is the ethic underlying the play and the views on religion it contains. The three principal characters, Nathan, the Knight Templar, and Saladin, are representatives of the three great religions, the Jewish, the Christian and the Moslem. Lessing's intention is to preach the doctrine of religious tolerance, a doctrine which had proved so foreign to his opponents in the recent controversy.[1] The finest representative of tolerance is Nathan himself, but the noble Saladin has no hesitation in appreciating and applauding Nathan's views and character. It is the Christian Templar who experiences the greatest difficulty in reaching Nathan's enlightened standpoint. The Templar has the Christian contempt for the Jewish race as strongly as the Baron in the earlier play, *The Jews*. "Willingly, most willingly I seized the opportunity to risk my life for that of another, even though it were only the life of a Jewess"[2] are the words with which the Templar rejects Nathan's grateful advances, after he has rescued the latter's adopted daughter, Recha. Though for a time he is converted to a more tolerant view by Nathan's forbearance and

---

[1] Goeze's intolerant denunciation of the Catholic faith involved him in 1779 in a diplomatic incident.

[2]   " Gern,
Sehr gern ergriff ich die Gelegenheit,
Es für ein andres Leben in die Schanze
Zu schlagen, für ein andres—wenn's auch nur
Das Leben einer Jüdin wäre." (ll. 1216–1220.)

generosity, yet he quickly relapses into his old hatred of
the Jews when Nathan's hesitation at according him the
hand of Recha (whom Nathan rightly suspects to be the
Templar's sister) arouses a suspicion against Nathan in
his mind. He consults the intolerant Christian Patriarch
and for an instant is on the point of denouncing the noble
Jew, when, at the last moment, the militant attitude of
this cleric makes him pause and averts the fearful consequences to which a betrayal of Nathan would have led.
Eventually the Templar too, after his many backslidings,
does succeed in attaining the tolerant attitude which
Nathan (and Lessing) advocates.

The Christian Templar is certainly a less noble character than Nathan, but he moves on the same plane.
Once he has realized the right course, he pursues it with
heart and soul. There is, however, another Christian
character, the Patriarch mentioned above, whose narrow,
intolerant, intriguing spirit illustrates the capacity of a
false conception of religion to blind the human mind to
the just and right course of action. The Patriarch with
his orthodox views and bigoted persecuting attitude[1]
is a projection of Goeze and his partisans. Lessing's
indignation, which threatened at first to manifest itself in
satirical form in the whole play, is concentrated in
Nathan in this single figure, who justifies his intrigues
with the statement—" what is knavery to men is not
knavery to God."[2]

Lessing's ethical system divides men into three
categories. First, there are those childlike characters
who are incapable of moral judgments ; such are the lay-
brother in this play, Recha's maid, Daja, and the Dervish.
Lessing can respect and love them, though they live upon
a lower plane than Nathan. Secondly, characters who
are capable of perceiving the right course and who yet do

[1] When the Templar consults him his eternal refrain is—" it matters not—the Jew shall be burned." ("Tut nichts ! der Jude wird verbrannt.") (Act IV, sc. ii.)

[2] " sei Bubenstück vor Menschen nicht auch Bubenstück vor Gott." (ll. 686-7).

not act upon it. These, of whom the Patriarch is representative, excite Lessing's strongest reprobation. The third and highest category is composed of those who, seeing what is right, act accordingly, because they feel they *must* do what is right. Such are Nathan and Saladin, and eventually the Templar.

Nathan is the key-figure to the play. All his actions, the result of mature reflection, are tolerant and generous. He is filled with the spirit of forbearance and charity. The insults of the Templar arouse in him no anger ;[1] he fills the treasury of Saladin unbidden ;[2] but the crowning proof of his charity is revealed in his narration of the circumstances which led to his adoption of Recha—his wife and seven sons had been massacred by Christians ; his grief was at first overwhelming—" Yet now reason gradually returned. It said with gentle voice, ' And yet God exists ! [and here Lessing's determinism appears] That too was God's will ! . . . ' I rose ! and called to God : 'I will ! Wilt thou that I will' ! "[3] The appearance of the forlorn Christian child seemed now a gift from God and Nathan adopted it as his own. For Nathan race and creed are indifferent— "are Christian and Jew Christian and Jew before they are men ? " he asks,[4] and the worth of a man is determined for him (and for Lessing) not by faith or creed or colour or the shape of a nose, but by his actions. Nathan's position, above the positive Jewish creed, dates from the recovery of his reason after the death of his wife and children. It is clear that Lessing had the loss of his own wife and child

---

[1] Act II, sc. v.

[2] Act III, sc. vii.

[3] " Doch nun kam die Vernunft allmählich wieder.
Sie sprach mit sanfter Stimm' : ' Und doch ist Gott !
Doch war auch Gottes Ratschluss das ! . . . .
. . . .
. . . . Ich stand ! und rief zu Gott : Ich will !
Willst du nur dass ich will ! " (ll. 3052–3059.)

[4] " Sind Christ und Jude eher Christ und Jude Als Mensch ? " (ll. 1310–1311).

in mind as he wrote this scene.[1]   It is not surprising,
therefore, to find here the profoundest expression of his
own attitude to religion, his faith in the purposes of God
and his realization of the necessity of submission to God's
will.   Nathan, like Lessing, has attained a comprehen-
sion of the truth of religion which enables him to dispense
with the outer trappings of any positive creed.

The relationship of these positive revealed religions to
the truth which underlay their dogmas, and which they
expressed cryptically (" all positive religions are true and
false in equal degree "), had occupied Lessing's mind
from the first conception of *Nathan the Wise*.   He had
hit upon a story of Boccaccio[2] which he thought would
serve the purpose of his play.   This story he embodied in
the vital scene of the third act (scene vii).   Saladin, who
expects a cunning and avaricious Jew, propounds a test
question :   Which of the three great religions is the true
one ?   Nathan's answer is a parable.   A father once
possessed a ring, which had " the secret power of making
the wearer, who believed in it, agreeable to God and
men."[3]   This father had three sons, whom he loved
equally ; being unwilling to favour only one, he had two
exact replicas of the ring made.   To each son he privately
gave a ring.   After the father's death the sons discovered
that each possessed a ring and a dispute arose as to which
was the true one ; for each maintained that he alone had
the true ring which he had received from his father's
hand.   But certainty was unattainable—" The true ring
proved undiscoverable.—Almost as undiscoverable as
the true faith is for us now,"[4] says Nathan, making his
first hint at the application of the parable.   Accordingly
the matter was brought before a judge.   This was the

---

[1] Act IV, sc. vii.

[2] *Decamerone, Giorn. I, Nov. 3.*

[3]   " die geheime Kraft, vor Gott
    Und Menschen angenehm zu machen, wer
    In dieser Zuversicht ihn trug."   (ll. 1915–7.)

[4]   " der echte Ring war nicht
    Erweislich :—Fast so unerweislich, als
    Uns itzt—der rechte Glaube."   (ll. 1962–4.)

verdict he pronounced : none of the rings was genuine.
The father presumably had three made instead of the
original one which was lost.[1] Yet each son should
attempt to prove that his own ring was the true one by
showing in his conduct that the secret power of the ring
was taking effect :

> Let each of you strive to reveal the virtue of the stone in his ring.
> Let each assist this virtue with gentleness, with heartfelt concilia-
> tion, with good works, with sincerest devotion to God ! If then the
> virtue of the stones appear with your children's children, then I
> summon them thousands of years hence once more before this seat
> of judgment.   A wiser man will then be sitting here to judge.[2]

Lessing intended this parable to bear the interpretation
that none of the positive revealed religions represents the
inmost truth ; that their forms are a matter of indifference
compared with the conduct they inspire in men.   The
parable is not a perfect vehicle for his meaning.   In
Boccaccio *one* of the rings was genuine and did really
convey the gift of being " agreeable to God and men."
For Lessing's message it is necessary that none of them
should be the true one, and he has thus to invest man
with the ability of attaining the effect of the ring by his
own efforts.   The possession of the true ring (the truth)
then becomes unimportant.   This technical defect,
though it is a flaw in the artistic structure of this scene,
does not obscure Lessing's meaning.   His plea for
tolerance and for virtuous conduct (justification by works)
rather than acknowledgment of a positive creed (justification by faith) emerges clearly from this central passage.
The most obvious feature of *Nathan the Wise* is its

---

[1] ll. 2023–2028.

[2] " Es strebe jeder von euch um die Wette,
Die Kraft des Steins in seinem Ring an Tag
Zu legen ! komme dieser Kraft mit Sanftmut,
Mit herzlicher Verträglichkeit, mit Wohltun,
Mit innigster Ergebenheit in Gott
Zu Hülf' ! Und wenn sich dann der Steine Kräfte
Bei euern Kindes-Kindern äussern,
So lad' ich über tausend tausend Jahre
Sie wiederum vor diesen Stuhl.   Da wird
Ein weisrer Mann auf diesem Stuhle sitzen
Als ich und sprechen."   (ll. 2043–2053.)

N

sincere and impassioned advocacy of religious tolerance. But, as we have seen, it contains far more than that. It embodies Lessing's profound faith in a religion of which the various positive religions are imperfect and transitory phases. The perception of this true religion is the wisdom of Nathan.

EPILOGUE

EPILOGUE

1. The Maker of Modern German Literature

Lessing's interests and activities were of the most diverse character. He remains unsurpassed in his versatility. He is that rare literary figure, the jack-of-all-trades and master of all. The extraordinary breadth of the field which he covered is in part responsible for the enormous influence he exercised on the literature of his age.

In 1750, when Lessing began his journalistic career, German literature was floundering purposelessly. It had neither tradition nor independence. A public, eager to read, but without guidance as to what it should read, applauded the diluted imitations of French works. Popular literature consisted of the pseudo-French classical tragedies sponsored by Gottsched, of comedies modelled on those of Destouches, and of the amiable and garrulous imitations of La Fontaine written by Gellert. One poet of power, Klopstock, the author of *The Messiah*, had certainly appeared ; but his work, in spite of the approval of the Swiss, met with vigorous opposition in Germany proper.

Thirty years later, German literature was the most flourishing in Europe. By 1780, the fervid enthusiasm of the period of *Storm and Stress* had produced plays of real power such as *Julius of Tarento* by Leisewitz and *The Soldiers* by Lenz. Goethe's *Götz von Berlichingen* had aroused the acclamation of the whole younger generation and his *Werther* had made a triumphal progress through all the countries of Western Europe. The very year of Lessing's death was to witness the appearance of still another writer of the first magnitude with the production of Schiller's *Robbers*, a work charged with vehement emotion at dangerously high tension. Twenty years later still, Coleridge and Scott in England and shortly afterwards Mme de Staël in France were to bring home to their readers the emergence of Germany as a first-class literary power.

At first sight Lessing's share in this florescence may not be apparent. He had withdrawn from active participation in literary life on his appointment to the post of Librarian in Wolfenbüttel. In *The Hamburg Dramaturgy* he had referred disparagingly to the dislike of criticism and contempt for the rules of art displayed by the rising generation, now known as the *Storm and Stress*. Only rarely did he refer to Goethe and not always with approval. But the first glance is here deceptive. Without Lessing, the *Storm and Stress* would at best have appeared twenty years later. Goethe and Schiller would have been seriously hampered in their development and neither could have written works of such power and originality as *Götz* and *The Robbers* while still scarcely more than youths. The whole course of German literature would, in short, have been altered. That they were able to produce mature works so early was due to Lessing's endeavours.

In 1750, German literature had no tradition; and without a tradition, without the guidance provided by an alert and critical mind and by a body of work which had the possibility of growth, not merely of imitation, Goethe and Schiller must have spent far more of their valuable and vital youthful powers than they actually did in the search for new forms. The creation of this tradition, as far as it lay in the power of any one man to do it, was Lessing's achievement.

Lessing saw that French classical literature was a foreign growth on German soil. Whatever its merits for the French type of mind and for the social conditions existing in France, it was ill-adapted to the requirements of the German with a totally different attitude of mind and in a totally different set of conditions. As long as the exaggerated admiration and respect for French work continued and as long as French authors remained the models for German writers, no German literature with originality and independence would arise. There was no possibility of growth. Through the years of Lessing's development this conviction evolved till it came to maturity in the seventeenth *Literaturbrief*. For the next ten years, Lessing's campaign against French taste was a decisive factor in German literature. Hardly had the immediate influence of the *Literaturbriefe* waned than a new impulsion came from *The Hamburg Dramaturgy*. Lessing himself expressed his scepticism as to the success of his campaign, but the works which were to appear in the 'seventies are abundant proof that his message had been read and absorbed by the new generation.

If this had been Lessing's only service to German literature it would still have been a valuable one ; he had cleared away the most formidable obstacle obstructing the natural development of German literature. But he did more than clear away. With unerring instinct he guided German literature, both in his criticism and in his plays, along the path which alone could lead to the production of a great literature.

Lessing was aware that no literature can be created suddenly and completely by the single fiat of a self-appointed dictator. It was not enough to shake off the artistic trammels of the French. For a time at any rate German literature must lean upon that of some more highly developed culture. The whole problem was to find such a literature, which would have some affinity to the German cast of mind, so that the natural development of the German mind would be helped rather than hindered. The solution lay in the popularization of English literature in Germany. The advocacy of English literature is the constructive complement to Lessing's attack on French taste from 1759 to 1769. The boundless admiration for Shakespeare, displayed by the writers of the *Storm and Stress* with Goethe at their head, is a consequence of Lessing's championship of the cause of English literature.

The imitation of a foreign literature, however much it

might be congenial to the German mind, was only a necessary but temporary phase. Lessing's ideal was an independent German literature, and he never failed to praise German work of originality and merit. Again and again he extols *The Messiah* of Klopstock, he commends Wieland's *Agathon* and shows great interest in the writings of Herder. When after 1770 his active part in critical journalism ceased, his work was already accomplished. He had orientated both the writers themselves and the public. The succeeding generation built on his foundations.

The effect of Lessing's plays was similar to that of his criticism. The condemnation of French classical principles was conveyed by implication, for these principles were ignored in the mature plays. Lessing drastically diminished the artificial and conventional elements which had hitherto characterized German drama (including his own early efforts). By the use of everyday characters in tragedy as well as comedy and by the natural tone of the prose dialogue he made the drama more " realistic " and renewed its contact with life at a time when it threatened to congeal into a formal pattern. The debt which Leisewitz's *Julius of Tarento* and Schiller's *Intrigue and Love* owe to Lessing's *Emilia Galotti* is obvious to the most casual glance. The influence of *Miss Sara Sampson* and of *Minna von Barnhelm* was also immense.

Lessing's historical achievement in furthering the development of German literature is less a matter of *finding* the right path than of choosing it and following it with single-minded persistence and energy. Few of his views were original; Bodmer and Breitinger had sung the praises of the English while Lessing was still in his infancy; models for his realistic plays were available in the work of Lillo and of Diderot; the basis of the aesthetic theories of the *Laocoon* was already stated in the writings of the Englishman Harris. No other writer of the period possessed, however, the energy, the tenacity and the determination to overcome all obstacles, which characterized Lessing's aggressive temperament. He alone among the self-appointed dictators of German literature had the qualities necessary both to maintain his position and to use it in the best interests of German literature. His resolute and often ruthless character enabled him to sustain his prestige while attacking the popular French taste in literature, while castigating incompetence and praising the work of new genius. He alone dominated German literature before the appearance of Goethe and he alone raised that literature in an age of mediocrity to the point at which the work of young Goethe and his contemporaries was possible. It says much that his prestige remained unaffected with succeeding generations, however much his absolute precepts might be neglected or rejected. The influence of his work was to extend even into the nineteenth century. Lessing is truly the founder of modern German literature.

2. Lessing Today

If Lessing had only been the critic and dramatist who laid the foundations for subsequent generations of German writers, he would still have merited respect and study. But he is more, far more than that. Our age still has much in common with him and still more to learn from him. His character and his mind, as they are exhibited in his works as well as in his life, command respect and admiration in a higher degree perhaps than those of any other German writer.

Lessing lived in an age of contrasts as sharp as those of our own day. Militant rationalists opposed militant theologians. Dogmatic critics of different schools elaborated and maintained contradictory systems which in no way corresponded to the facts and needs of literature. Theoretical politicians formulated systems without heeding the possibilities and conditions of their time. In this welter of conflicting opinions Lessing's view is always characterized by sound common-sense. He is free from the exaggeration and the doctrinaire attitude of so many of his contemporaries. His attacks on French taste in Germany did not blind him to the merits of the greatest French authors. His praise of Klopstock did not obscure the latter's faults. He recognized the power of *Werther*, though he objected to its morality. This sane common-sense is conspicuously applied to his Biblical studies. His clear head and freedom from prejudice enable him to approach the subject without bias in either direction. His dispassionate examination of the Synoptic Gospels is the first important scientific attempt to investigate their origin. All Lessing's predecessors had had some point to prove or axe to grind. He alone saw with an impartial eye and noted down with sober clarity the results of his conscientious research.

Sanity is the keynote, too, of Lessing's political views and observations. Very early (1751) he had shown a healthy and reasonable antipathy to Rousseau's praise of the warlike spirit.[1] In the *Literaturbriefe* he was to show eight years later that his pacifism was marked by plain sense and an absence of unpractical theorizing, for in the fifth Letter he disposes of an eighteenth-century proposition for a " League of Nations " and " sanctions " on the ground that one recalcitrant nation can involve the others in war and so produce the very result which the scheme sought to avoid.[2] Instead, Lessing gives a qualified approval to a project of gradual disarmament. A striking instance of Lessing's moderation is his play *Emilia Galotti*. Its theme afforded facile opportunities for the denunciation of the despotism of petty courts as it existed in the eighteenth century. Less than ten years later Schiller was to use a similar subject for a vehement denunciation of the conditions of the courts. Lessing abstains from any attempt to point the moral. He concerns himself only with the human problems and

[1] PO. 8, 30.   [2] PO. 4, 31-2.

leaves the spectator to draw what conclusion he will about the political implications.

The most striking expression of Lessing's political views occurs towards the end of his life in his masonic dialogues, *Ernst und Falk*. This work consists of five dialogues of which the first three were published by Lessing in 1778, whilst the last two were issued without his consent two years later. The Free-masons appear in these dialogues as men who seek to surmount the barriers which state and society erect between various nations and classes. They seek to "make what are generally called good deeds superfluous."[1] In the fourth dialogue, Lessing made it clear that he did not approve of the Lodges of his day and considered that membership was immaterial to the attainment of the ethical standpoint which seemed to him to be the basis of Free-masonry.

This conception of the social significance of Free-masonry leads Lessing to consider the state of his day. He has no sympathy with the idea of the state as an entity existing apart from its members. Twice he expressly affirms that the state is a means for the happiness of the individual and that the happiness of the state is the sum total of the happiness of its members and not its conquests or material prosperity, unless these contribute to the happiness of all the individuals. Lessing rejects socialism as impracticable, for the whole of society is founded on the paradox "that men can only be united by separation."[2] Lessing's sanity appears most clearly, however, in his attitude to patriotism. He recognizes that it has a value, yet he considers that there is a point where it ceases to be a virtue.[3] His critical writings show how he deplored the sorry state of German cultural life ; but he had no sympathy with the nationalism

[1] " Was man gemeiniglich gute Taten zu nennen pflegt, entbehrlich zu machen." (PO. 6, 29. MK. 7, 371.)

[2] " die Menschen sind nur durch Trennung zu vereinigen." (PO. 6, 35. MK. 7, 381.)

[3] PO. 6, 36. MK. 7, 382.

which insists on territorial expansion and wars of aggression.

Lessing appeals most obviously to readers of today through the insistent pleas for religious and racial tolerance which occur throughout his work. In his early twenties the play, *The Jews*, had shown his deep antipathy to the unreasonable hatred directed against that people. Thirty years later at the end of his life, *Nathan the Wise* proved that his convictions had not weakened. His advocacy of tolerance is not confined to Jews alone. He pleads for the Moravians, for a Unitarian such as Neuser, and for heretics of all descriptions. His spirit of tolerance is all the more valuable because it is not, as it is with Frederick the Great, the outcome of religious indifference. It is the positive consequence of his convictions, not the negative result of the lack of them. Its root is to be found in the high value he sets on the noblest qualities of man, and in his unprejudiced realization that these qualities are not limited by creed or colour. Here as elsewhere Lessing saw with his own eyes.

Only a very few years ago, Lessing's tolerance must have seemed to Englishmen of historical interest only, as it had long been the common property of civilized men. How far this was from the truth, recent events have demonstrated. The spirit of tolerance is more lacking today than in the eighteenth century; and Lessing's noble message is of greater importance than ever before.

On religious or political subjects, as on every other, Lessing never loses his sense of proportion. The exaggeration of one single aspect of the matter on hand, so characteristic of German critics and thinkers, is no feature of his work. He always sees his problem in its entirety and never elevates detail above the whole. He is never dazzled by brilliant theories, nor led from the point by irrelevant digressions. His sound common-sense wins and retains the confidence of his readers.

Lessing's sense of proportion is indeed one of his most salient characteristics, but it is a less obvious one than his passion for accuracy. In an age when slipshod habits of thought and language are more rife than ever before, Lessing's insistence on precision bears a message. The negative side of his love of exactitude appears in his severity against bad translation, as with Lange and Lieberkühn. The attacks on Klotz,[1] on Dusch[2] and on Gregorius,[3] prove that he was equally stringent in his views on the loose use of language. He was the sworn enemy of tautologies, of periphrases and of euphemisms. He used the normal word, called a spade a spade, and hated all unnecessary expenditure of breath. Lessing cites Aristotle with approval as a " saver of words,"[4] and he himself was as economical with them as the clear expression of his meaning would permit.

Lessing was not only accurate in style and exact in translation. The same quality marks his scholarship. His facts are always as correct as the facilities of research available to him will allow. His deductions are based on ascertained facts and proceed almost always without any leaps into the fanciful. If his views are now in many cases rejected, it is because the range of available facts has been extended since his day. His conscientious thoroughness, coupled with vigour and energy, are a model of scholarly method.

Lessing's accurate use of words and of facts is allied to a style of remarkable clarity. His critical and theological work can be read for the pure pleasure of its incisive, downright mode of writing. He handles dialectic with skill and carries his readers easily along the course of an intricate argument. He is particularly brilliant at resolving a logical process into a dialogue, a device which obviously makes for greater clarity and facility of

---

[1] *Briefe antiquarischen Inhalts.*

[2] *Literaturbriefe*, 41.

[3] *Beyträge zur Historie und Aufnahme des Theaters.*

[4] " Wortsparer," *Hamburgische Dramaturgie*, 77, Stück. (PO. 5, 321. MK. 5, 261.)

understanding.[1] He has the gift of making the most abstruse problems clear to the man in the street ; often light is suddenly thrown on a complex question by a vivid image, which even the most obtuse could comprehend.

Above all, Lessing's style is noteworthy for its extreme relevance. It is always concise, always bearing on the subject, never discursive or evocative. He is a supreme master of prose not as a form of fine art in itself, but as a means for the exposition of thought in the best possible way. His style is perfectly adapted to his purpose in his critical and theological work.

Lessing's passion for accuracy, his sanity and his clear and emphatic mode of writing make of him the perfect journalist. His profound conscientiousness preserves him from the risk of unfounded assertion, whilst his vivid style ensures a most readable article. His journalistic work may be read with interest almost in its entirety even today, a remarkable compliment to the soundness of its matter and the quality of its style. Lessing possessed the journalist's talent of writing vividly on any subject, but it was the invariable accuracy of his information and soundness of his views which placed him head and shoulders above all journalists of his age. At the same time the journalistic gift came to the assistance of Lessing's sound and precise knowledge in another field. If Lessing was the perfect journalist, he was also the perfect scholar. He had the necessary thoroughness, the breadth of reading and of view, and the love of exactitude. But he had also the gift of making his subject live. No one can read such works as *Berengar of Tours* or the *Rehabilitation of Cochläus* without feeling how vivid the subject is for Lessing himself and how successful he is in communicating his interest to the reader. Yet the vividness of his style never involves him in any sacrifice of truth, any more than the weightiness of the matter or the passion for accuracy detracts from the

[1]*Das Testament Johannis, Ernst und Falk* and Fragments.

liveliness of his style. It is so often assumed that journalists must be superficial and that scholars must be dull that the example of Lessing is particularly salutary, for he combined in the same person the qualities necessary for journalism and for scholarship and showed that the fusion of these qualities produced work of an exceptionally high order in both these spheres.

Another characteristic of Lessing helped to make his scholarship live. He always maintained contact with the present. History is not for him a question purely of the discovery of facts, but of the lessons which the present age may deduce from those facts. He may even have a more immediate goal, as in *Adam Neuser*, where he uses the history of Neuser to challenge the attitude of the orthodox clergy. Yet he is proof against the temptation to distort, which this application of history to the present frequently involves. He is aware of the continuity of history and investigates it in a scientific spirit, not seeking to adapt it to a preconceived theory, but to discover the principles underlying its course.

The conception of the pure scholar who has no interest in the use to which his research is put was entirely foreign to Lessing. The application of his historical investigations to his own day was only one aspect of his constructive cast of mind. As a critic and as a theologian, Lessing certainly destroyed much, but he never halted there, he always went further and offered something constructive in place of what he had destroyed. This extraordinary constructive urge is one of the most striking and one of the most valuable of Lessing's characteristics. Time after time he demolishes an obsolete standpoint and each time he has some positive suggestion to make in its stead. In the seventeenth *Literaturbrief* the pseudo-French classicism of Gottsched is rejected, but English literature and above all Shakespeare are proposed as substitutes. In the *Treatises on the Fable*, Lessing begins by showing the inadequacy of previous definitions, but he does not fail to conclude by giving a definition himself.   These are only two examples ; but they could be multiplied almost indefinitely.   Lessing is an architect as well as a house-breaker.

Lessing's controversial writings are noteworthy for their unusually constructive character. Polemical writings tend so easily to degenerate into mere personal feuds that it is really remarkable to note how Lessing, even in his most virulent essays, always retains a clear view of his goal and directs his energies to a practical end.   The destructive power which, at a superficial glance, is his salient characteristic, assumes on closer inspection the proportions of a necessary but temporary phase.   Lessing's work is never complete until he has abandoned the negative for the positive, demolition for construction.   The energy and scope of his mind become more apparent when one considers that he combines in superlative degree two tendencies which are almost invariably separated.

Lessing always pursues his aim without hesitation or swerving.   In a sense he is an opportunist.   He is quick to seize upon every possible occasion for the furtherance of his aim, but his pursuit of the aim never falters.   No one ever succeeded in side-tracking him ; for he was of all writers the one to whom relevance was most valuable. This interest in the subject, which compels his strict adherence to the matter on hand, is a consequence of Lessing's profound sincerity.   The numerous controversies in which he was involved shed a brilliant light on his upright and candid character.   No writer of note has shared in such numerous and fierce disputes as Lessing ; yet there is no suspicion of a personal motive as the occasion of a dispute.   It was the *work* of Lange, of Dusch, of Lieberkühn and of Klotz which aroused Lessing's anger.   Their private life and their personal qualities lay outside his sphere.   Even in the theological conflict, which Lessing so ardently desired, his motive was the hope of clarification resulting from the interchange of contradictory views.   Lessing's singleness of mind and purpose is the more apparent when he is compared with another great controversialist of his century, Voltaire. Voltaire valued victory above all else ; he could never entirely succeed in dissociating the pursuit of truth from all personal motives. Lessing's blunt character, devoid of the slightest trace of vanity, succeeded where Voltaire failed. Lessing realized that the discovery of the truth benefits the defeated in literary, philosophical or scientific controversy as much as it benefits the victorious. In civil cases a litigant may profit by the ignorance of his opponent, " because," says Lessing in the *Rehabilitation of Cardanus*, " his loss is necessarily involved in the other's gain. . . . However, this is not so in disputes which have truth for their object . . . whichever party wins does not win for itself alone. The party which loses, loses nothing but errors and can at any moment share in the victory of the other. Honesty is therefore what I demand first and foremost from a philosopher."[1] Honesty is in fact the characteristic of Lessing's writings whether in controversy or in the exposition of his thought.

This integrity and purity of motive makes Lessing's combative literary career comprehensible and admirable. At first sight he may appear quarrelsome, and savagely aggressive—a provocative bully, with an entertainingly satirical pen. How far such a view would be from the truth I have sought to show. Lessing was provocative only on one subject, theology ; and the motive underlying this provocation was, as we have seen, he desire to arrive by way of controversy at a clear conception of the truth. Lessing's virulence is a consequence of his determination to pursue his path to its ultimate goal, regardless of whatever opposition might arise against

---

[1] " Weil sein Verlust notwendig mit des andern Gewinne verbunden ist, . . . Dieses aber findet sich bei den Streitigkeiten, welche die Wahrheit zum Vorwurfe haben, nicht . . . es mag sie der eine oder der andre Teil gewinnen, so gewinnt er sie doch nie für sich selbst. Die Partei, welche verlieret, verlieret nichts als Irrtümer und kann alle Augenblicke an dem Siege der andern teilnehmen. Die Aufrichtigkeit ist daher das erste, was ich an einem Weltweisen verlange." (PO. 20, 121).

him ; his bitterest attacks are reserved for those who
obscure the issue by raising personal questions and
accusations which are totally irrelevant to the matter
under discussion. It was Lessing's misfortune that
almost all of his opponents in controversy were of
inferior moral calibre. Again and again they diverted
the controversy into personal channels ; Lessing's
victory was easy, but the pursuit of truth in these disputes
was one-sided and rested solely upon his efforts.

Lessing's sincerity of purpose appears in his manner of
life. He set no store on the goods of this world. So he
praised Nicolai for his decision to live by his pen, saying,
" as long as you can live it does not matter whether you
live on a large or small income,"[1] and Lessing himself
valued his time (" all that I possess "[2]) above everything.
Provided that he could live without great hardship, and
had time for his literary work and research Lessing was
content. The profits of his one remunerative post in
Breslau were applied to the relief of his family and the
acquisition of a library. One thing alone mattered to
him—the leisure to pursue his studies. Social advancement did not interest him ; he detested the flattering,
hypocritical politeness it required. He was convinced of
his duty and his aim in life ; and he lived accordingly,
never sacrificing what he conceived to be the right course
to his personal comfort or advancement.

Lessing lived and died a poor and solitary man. But
no note of self-pity ever crossed his lips. He lived his
life resolutely and courageously. The heroic gesture and
the imposing phrase were alike foreign to him. He
cared nothing for the opinion of others so long as his own
conscience sanctioned his conduct. Both in his life and
in his works he appears as a sincere, outspoken and
determined man who went his own way. So great were
the power of his mind and the sanity of his judgment that
that way was to prove the salvation of German literature

[1] Letter of 29th November, 1756.

[2] Letter to Mendelssohn of 30th March, 1761.

from the impasse to which it had come in the earlier part of the eighteenth century.

Lessing's independence of mind, penetrative power, breadth of interest and freedom from prejudice make of him the most admirable figure in the history of German thought and literature between Luther and Nietzsche. He possessed their energy and he surpassed them in the sane robustness of his views. He matters to us most of all now as a man of admirable personal qualities, who was wholly enwrapped in his task, presents no subtle psychological problems and never intrudes irrelevant personal elements into his work. Lessing is certainly always completely himself in his work, yet such is the integrity of his personality that the reader is unaware of any personal element. His character is bound up with his work, and his work is an aspect of his character. No German writer has ever surpassed him in this integrity and singleness of purpose. He is not only the founder of modern German literature ; the qualities which appear in his work are still an inspiration a hundred and fifty years after his death. Lessing would have desired no better judgment than this, which he amply deserves :

He was a man, take him for all in all.

BIBLIOGRAPHICAL NOTE

(1) EDITIONS

Lessings Werke, 25 Parts, edited by J. Petersen and W. v. Olshauser Bong & Co.

Lessings sämtliche Schriften, 23 Volumes, edited by Muncker, after Lachmann's text. Leipzig, 1886–1924.

(2) GENERAL WORKS

W. Dilthey : *Das Erlebnis und die Dichtung*, Chaps. I–V. 1905.

W. Oehlke : *Lessing und seine Zeit*, 2 vols. 1919.

T. W. Rolleston : *Life of G. E. Lessing*. London. 1899.

E. Schmidt : *Lessing*. 2 vols. 3rd Edn. 1909.

C. Schrempf : *Lessing*. 1913 (*Aus Natur und Geisteswelt*).

J. Sime : *Lessing, his Life and Works*. 2 vols. 1877.

A. M. Wagner : *Lessing*. 1931.

B. v. Wiese : *Lessing*. 1931.

(3) SPECIAL WORKS

The following are particularly worthy of note :—

G. Fittbogen : *Die Religion Lessings*. 1923.

G. Kettner : *Lessings Dramen im Lichte ihrer und unserer Zeit*. 1907.

H. Leisegang : *Lessings Weltanschauung*. 1931.

R. Petsch : *Lessings Faustdichtung*. 1911.

C. Schrempf : *Lessings al Philosoph*. 1921.

INDEX